# THE CHILD FIGURE
# IN ENGLISH LITERATURE

# The
# Child Figure
# in English Literature

ROBERT PATTISON

ATHENS
THE UNIVERSITY OF GEORGIA PRESS

Library of Congress Catalog Card Number: 76–2893
International Standard Book Number: 0–8203–0409–3
The University of Georgia Press, Athens 30602
Copyright © 1978 by the University of Georgia Press
All rights reserved
Set in 11 on 14 point Times Roman type
Printed in the United States of America

Alas, regardless of their doom,
The little victims play!

Gray, "Ode on a Distant Prospect
of Eton College"

# Contents

# Preface

This book is about the conjunction of a literary figure—the child—and two ideas fundamental to Western culture—the concepts of the Fall of Man and of Original Sin.

When I began to examine the child in English literature, largely with the object of understanding the Victorian interest in preadolescence, I was struck by something peculiarly un-Victorian in the treatment of children: with a frequency too routine to be coincidental, they would turn up, not in the family environment but as solitary, isolated figures against backgrounds of social and philosophic melancholy. The nursery with its sturdy toys, the readings in front of the hearth before the circular kisses and good nights, even the dose of laudanum administered to still the wailing infant by proletarian mother and society nanny alike—in short, the domestic paraphernalia of Victorian life seemed lacking in the depiction of childhood. And in its place was a succession of graveyards and wonderlands where the child wandered alone; even when the child possessed a family, as in *Dombey and Son,* the sense of beleaguered detachment seemed to overshadow any domesticity.

To account for this bleak consistency in the literary presentation of children, I looked back through the eighteenth century, through the seventeenth, through the Renaissance and medieval periods to find a source for the later use of the child figure. The further I receded from

the modern period, the scantier were the references to.
children, yet at the same time, the clearer the contexts in
which they appeared: the early depiction of childhood in
English literature is generally characterized by specific
mention of baptism and sin, and the earliest portraits are
clearly theological in bearing.

With this understanding, it required little effort to dis-
cern Augustine on the horizon, and the following pages
will trace the connection between the debates of the early
Church over the definition of man's fallen condition, in
which, after Augustine, the child figured so prominently,
and the later development of the literary figure.

I do not mean to imply in this book that all works
containing children are solely about the Fall of Man or
that all children in all English literature are spokesmen
for Augustine and the dogma of Original Sin which he
propounded. But the frequency with which children appear in literary surroundings which discuss man's fallen
nature (and the surprising tendency of these discussions
to support the orthodox position of the Church) suggests
at least the premise that the child figure in English literature generally appears in thematic surroundings which
discuss the Fall of Man, and that the norm against which
we have become accustomed to measure these discussions
is the Christian doctrine of Original Sin.

In demonstrating this premise, I have set certain
boundaries to the scope of the book in order to keep
the argument as compact and manageable as possible.
This work is not a survey of all children in all English
literature: such an undertaking would require a far length-
ier book. I have restricted myself to English writers (Henry
James is included by his own choice) writing before World

War I. I have avoided educational tracts, an area of immense scope which bears only tangentially upon the literary figure of the child. And I have omitted references in English literature to the Christ child, whose presentation presents questions concerned not so much with childhood and the Fall as with the whole range of Christian belief.

I hope these are not the omissions of indolence or obfuscation. The works excluded from discussion by these limitations might be used to write a second volume with the same theme as this one, and indeed, I have been sorely tempted to make the obvious application of this book's premise to Hawthorne and Twain; to include a discussion of that most Augustinian work, *A High Wind in Jamaica;* or to draw the nymphic parallels between the wonderlands of Lewis Carroll and Nabokov's *Lolita*. The list of possibilities is almost endless, but I have restrained myself in the hope that the material provided here is sufficient to enable a reader to go, with a fresh perspective, to any work which employs the child figure.

If I have accomplished this or anything else here, I owe a great debt to John Rosenberg of Columbia University, without whose patience and discernment at every line of the original copy this book would be shape without form, and in the revisions and decisions which have accompanied this work, I have relied heavily on the advice and support of E. Mason Cooley and Alan Shaw. To them I want to offer my thanks.

ROBERT PATTISON

# THE CHILD FIGURE
# IN ENGLISH LITERATURE

# I

# The Child Figure
# From Homer to Augustine

Hector's son ran screaming to his nurse's arms when his warrior father put on his bronze helmet topped with a horseplume. Hector quickly put aside the offending helmet and fondled the child in his arms, while Andromache, smiling through tears of grief for her husband's departure, gathered the young Astyanax to her fragrant breast.[1]

Remarkable as the first child in classical literature, Astyanax is more remarkable for the modernity with which he is presented. He is not only one of a handful of children who appear in Western writing before comparatively recent times, but one of the very few whose treatment is marked by the touches of delicacy and sentiment which become the hallmark of children depicted after the seventeenth century. In contrast to the Homeric and modern attitudes, Greek and Roman writers generally ignored the child as a subject, and when they do mention children, it is almost invariably as subrational, subhuman creatures outside the pale of literary interest. "Both children and the lower animals share in voluntary action, but not in choice,"[2] remarks Aristotle, lumping beasts and children together, just as earlier in the *Ethics* he had excluded both groups from the possession of virtue or happiness: "Boys who are called happy are being congratulated by reason of the hopes we have for them,"[3] he states, indicating that the child is to be regarded as a potential but not an actual human being because he is devoid of reason.

The Stoics set fourteen as the age at which a child came into possession of reason, and it is no coincidence that they picked a year in the flush of puberty. The onslaught of sexuality was regarded as a physical symptom of the developing inner bud of reason. This point is made in works as disparate as Plato's *Phaedrus* and Petronius's *Satyricon,* both of which hinge on the youthful and immature corruption of physical love seen as a reflection of an analogous and equally immature corruption of reason—reason in each case being expressed through its art, rhetoric. The Greek and Roman cultures prized maturity above all else. They loved to think of man at the high point as he turned on the wheel of life, in the full vigor of action and passion. They froze their gods in a mature eternity and dwelt as little as they could on Zeus's swaddling clothes. The first Homeric hymn to Hermes tells how the god was born at dawn, played the lyre by midday, and stole the cattle of Apollo by evening. Hermes' delirious maturity is typical of the Greek impatience with childhood.

Vergil's Ascanius, as befits the imperial epic, is more dignified than Hector's son but less interesting in himself. To give the child substance and purpose, Vergil makes him the object of a fiery portent from the gods,[4] a gesture which reinforces the Aristotelian concept that the child is important not for himself but for his potential; Ascanius is interesting because of his destiny and that of Rome. Cato the Elder's son appears in Plutarch as a foil to his father's republican virtues, while Roman schools in the first century of the empire set young children the same mechanical, unreasoning assignments the modern world reserves for lunatics—repetitious measuring, counting, and reciting. Quintilian thought of children as "vessels with narrow mouths," [5] empty creatures into whom the soul of grammar and oratory is to be poured once they break out of the shell of childhood.

A subtler idea of childhood, implied in parts of Platonic philosophy and perhaps derived from elements of Pythagorean doctrine, gives the child a curious kind of importance by making him the vehicle in which the transmigrating soul resides. This does not mean that Plato has any more patience with children than Aristotle; in the *Laws,* he says, "Of all animals, the boy is the most unmanageable; inasmuch as he has the fountain of reason in him not yet regulated, he is an insidious and sharp-witted animal and the most insubordinate of them all." [6] The *Republic* is an attempt to correct this bestial condition of childhood in the most reasonable way. But while Plato shared the general Greek disdain for childhood, his philosophy, implicitly at least, requires a more optimistic evaluation of childhood than that voiced in the *Laws.* The theory of Innate Ideas in the *Phaedo* necessarily makes the infant the repository of the Ideas in their purest form, since the child has come directly from the realm of Ideas. This picture is interestingly elaborated in a passage from the *Timaeus:*

> But when the current of growth and nutriment flows in less strongly, and the revolutions, taking advantage of the calm, once more go their way and become yet more settled as time goes on, thenceforward the revolutions are corrected to the form that belongs to the several

circles in their natural motion; and giving their right
names to what is different and to what is the same,
they set their possessor in the way to become rational.
And now if some right nurture lends help towards
education, he becomes entirely whole and unblemished,
having escaped the worst of maladies; whereas if he be
neglectful, he journeys through a life halt and maimed
and comes back to Hades uninitiate and without
understanding.[7]

Before he is rational, the child is a chaotic assortment of
unsettled motions and revolutions, but as these motions
find their proper orbit, corresponding to the revolutions
of the heavens, reason naturally appears, like Adam in
the garden, "giving their right names to what is different
and to what is the same." With proper education, detailed in the *Republic,* the rational soul has the capability
to become "entirely whole and unblemished." In other
words, the chaotic state of childhood contains in it the
possibility of human, rational perfection, and the attain-
ment of this goal is entirely within the reach of human
effort. If the soul is condemned to return to Hades "uninitiate and without understanding," the failure has been
one of human omission and neglect.

Plato's optimistic evaluation of the chances for human
perfection, together with the picture of the reasonless but
potentially unblemished child which lies behind it, may
have been challenged by a classical theory of Original Sin
derived from the Orphic cult.[8] But if a concept of Original
Sin did exist in the classical mind, it was not powerful
enough to stimulate the elaborate mechanisms of expiation
which come with the Christian notion of universal Fall
and personal responsibility. And not only did it fail to
produce the confessor or the analyst, but it also seems

not to have generated the climate of intense debate in which the Church reserves the word *heresy* for the loser. Eight hundred years after Plato, Pelagius undoubtedly was speaking in the best and the virtually unchallenged tradition of Greek thought when he proclaimed the perfectibility of the reasonable man without the aid of God's prevenient grace. But by then his position represented a threat to the mythic and dogmatic unity of the Christian faith, which came to demand not a philosophy of perfectibility which men might choose if they pleased, but a religion joining all mankind in pervasive and original error—error not reasonably committed by rational adults but residing in the will even of infants. In this inclusive, religious view of the original nature of man, in which the accent has been shifted from reason to will as the primary object and vehicle of human melioration, the child rose to a station of great importance.

The ancient world had no corresponding faith and no corresponding idea of the child's significance. Plato's myth confirms the idea of the child as reasonless and sees in him the potential for perfection. Much the same thinking probably lies behind the mythic figure of Cupid, whose impish pranks in infancy work a havoc of irrationality in gods and men alike similar to the erratic revolutions of the child soul before it attains reason, but whose maturity is lived out in the perfection of his marriage to Psyche.

Certainly the most striking feature of classical literature's attitude toward children is the thunderous silence that envelops the idea of childhood, especially when compared to the outpouring of concern and attention recent centuries have produced on the same subject. The classical silence does not necessarily indicate indifference. While Roman infants might be subject to death by exposure and were largely neglected before they came to a reasonable age, the Roman child wore the purple-striped toga of rank and dignity throughout his childhood, exchanging it only at puberty for the *toga virilis*. This strange aura of distinction surrounding the otherwise overlooked child almost certainly stems from the potential for glory and perfection thought to be lodged within the child's still unreasoning being. Andromache's tender sympathies for Astyanax may have been the rule in classical society, but for a writer to dwell on these sentiments was indeed exceptional. Childhood raised few questions and evoked only the slenderest train of associations. The child may have contained the possibility of perfection, but until the possibility bore actual fruit, he remained subreasonable and therefore subliterary.

Plutarch's letter to his wife on the death of their young daughter Timoxena demonstrates what seems to us the ambivalence between sentiment and indifference in the classical approach to children. After speaking of the "pure pleasure" and "the very special kind of poignancy about the love we feel for such very young children," he ends his letter by reminding his wife of the good sense behind the traditional attitude toward the death of children: "It is not our way to pour out libations for children who die in infancy nor to perform the other ceremonies which the living do for the dead. This is because these infants are in no way involved with earth or earthly things; and so people do not stand around long at their funerals or keep watch at the tombs or at the laying out or at the side of the bodies."[9] In Plutarch, the "unearthly" quality of childhood has only a trace of the significance it will assume in Christian literature. For him the loss of Timoxena is easier precisely because she is unearthly, just as a statue would be better lost in the earlier stages of its creation than at its completion. "Unearthly" is for Plutarch an expression connoting the lack of fulfillment. When the Church and early Christian writers made the idea of the unearthly convey a sense of realization and fulfillment, the child naturally acquired a higher degree of prestige and importance than Plutarch is able to attach to his daughter.

Horace devotes an entire ode to a discussion of the unearthliness of the young girl Lalage, who, though portrayed in a very natural and earthy setting, is not a part of the scene around her because of her lack of reason and sexuality. This is the only classical work of distinction which uses and develops the child figure,[10] and here the little girl is used only to be dismissed till her maturity:

> Nondum subacta ferre iugum valet
> Cervice, nondum munia comparis
>     Aequare nec tauri ruentis
>         In venerem tolerare pondus.
> Circa virentis est animus tuae
> Campos iuvencae, nunc fluviis gravem
>     Solantis aestum, nunc in udo
>         Ludere cum vitulis salicto
> Praegestientis.      (*Odes* 2.5.1–9)

(She is not yet strong enough to bear the yoke on her submitting neck, nor is she equal to the duties of a wife or ready to bear the weight of the love-struck bull who rushes toward her. Your young girl's spirit is abroad in the green fields, warding off the oppressive heat among its streams and eager to frolic with the bull-calfs in the reedy marsh.)

Horace's young girl is surrounded not only by nature, but by explicitly sexual metaphor. It is one of the destinies of young girls in literature that their innocence should be seen only in light of its loss. From the first word of the ode. Horace emphasizes the classical feeling that nature, like man, is best at its prime. The girl is not yet (*nondum*) ready. Latent sexuality is no more fascinating than the latent manhood of Hector's son, and the poem shifts to the girl's potential sexuality, to the coming time when

> iam proterva
> Fronte petet Lalage maritum.
> (15–16)

(Bold to the point of forwardness, Lalage will look for a husband.)

Like Aristotle before him, Horace at first places the child among the animals, then looks forward to a time when it will be mature. But Horace shows us the young girl playing with the animals in a way that is at once delightful and disturbing. The picture of natural harmony summoned up by the young Lalage's sporting with the calf by the river bank is darkened by the recognition that this calf is a bull-calf, *vitulus,* who will grow up to be the *taurus* of the first stanza. To the Christian mind, the darkness of the passage lies in the sexual threat to innocence, the young child courting her approaching doom, as Marvell's nymph loved her faun. But to Horace the darkness lies not in the future, when Lalage will find herself a husband and presumably fulfill her sexual promise, herself, and her social function, but in the *nondum,* in the incompleteness of the girl's situation, in her association with the animals which makes her humanity ambiguous.

This theme of ambiguity is echoed in the poem's final stanza, and is properly the subject of the poem:

> Cnidiusve Gyges,
> Quem si puellarum insereres choro,
> Mire sagacis falleret hospites
> Discrimen obscurum solutis
> Crinibus ambiguoque voltu.
> (20–24)

(Cnidian Gyges, who, if you dropped him in the midst of maidens, would fool the sharp wits of those who did not know him, hidden as he is behind long hair and looks that might belong to either sex.)

Horace makes the point that Lalage will be a greater delight in her maturity than Gyges, who seems half-boy, half-girl. Ambiguity is a threat. When Lalage attains her full unambiguous sexual nature, then her humanity will have come to fruition and she will marry, contributing to the civilized, rational life of man. Whatever Horace's beauties, they are not Wordsworth's.

Needless to say, Christian writers could not feel quite the same distaste for childhood when they finally came to treat the subject:

> Happy those early dayes! when I
> Shin'd in my Angell-infancy.
> Before I understood this place
> Appointed for my second race
> Or taught my soul to fancy ought
> But a while, Celestiall thought.
> ("The Retreate," 1–6)

What is remarkable is not that Christian authors like Vaughan made use of children and changed the substance of the classical picture of childhood, but that they took centuries to do it. In light of Jesus' references to children, the delay in adopting a new stance toward them calls for an explanation.

"Suffer the little children and forbid them not to come unto me, for of such is the kingdom of heaven" (Matt. 19:14), Christ had said, and Jewish tradition stood behind him to give scope and dimension to the role of the child. The child Samuel ministered to the Lord before Eli (1 Sam. 3), the people of Israel were the children of the living God (Ps. 82:6), and the rite of circumcision inducted the infant into the community as at a much later age the *toga virilis* brought the young man into Roman society, although the rite of circumcision lays its primary stress on the humanity and Jewishness of the child, relegating to a secondary place the function of reason as a criterion for judging of human capacity.

The Old Testament contains at least the germ of the idea from which the Christian dogma of Original Sin develops. The God of Genesis curses Adam and his progeny for Adam's disobedience and, surveying humanity after the Flood, remarks that "the imagination of man's heart is evil from his youth" (8:21). The psalmist goes even further: "Behold, I was shapen in iniquity; and in sin did my mother conceive me" (51:5). But however much children were recognized as the equals of adults, especially as regarded their sins, Jewish tradition never made them the focal point of any doctrinal issue as the Christians later did, and the peculiar mixture of suffrance and wrath which the Church visited upon the young is nowhere to be found in the Old Covenant. When the children mocked Elisha on his journey to Bethel, calling out, "Go up, thou bald head," the prophet did them the honor of treating them exactly like adults and cursed them in the name of the Lord: "And there came forth two she bears out of the wood, and tare forty and two children of them" (2 Kings 2:24).

Under the New Covenant, circumcision, the fleshy act of the law, is replaced by baptism, wherein a man receives God's grace and enters the Church of Christ. But in the early Church the rite of baptism was not only the outward and visible sign of an inward and spiritual grace, but of a fundamental conflict over the nature, direction, and purpose of the new religion. This conflict came to a head (though not to a resolution) in the debate between Augustine and Pelagius.

During the course of the debate over the Pelagian heresy, the child firmly established itself as an enduring element of Christian thought, whose importance, however minimal socially, could not be overlooked theologically. Nor has the child as a figure of dogmatic and literary importance ever escaped from the influence of those sister heresies which engaged the Church during the period when children became the objects of theological scrutiny. In later chapters, the child figure will be seen in many contexts which call to mind the Gnostic, Manichean, and Arian debates of the early Church. The Pelagian heresy touches on each of these others at least peripherally, and the following discussion is therefore limited to the child's role in the development of the dogma of Original Sin.

Pelagius himself, the author of the heresy which Augustine defeated by clarifying his own thought and seeing it become dogma, was a dignified and retiring personality of almost Hellenistic sensibility. He never met his great antagonist, and unlike his coheretic Caelestius who flung himself into the fray with a zeal that suggests fanaticism, he seems to have preferred studious retreat and the quiet company of devout friends. He attended none of the councils at which he was denounced and appears to have been stunned when his excommunication came in 418. Suddenly deserted by his friends and branded by the Church he loved as an enemy, he probably finished out his life in Egyptian exile, producing a commentary on the Song of Solomon and perhaps (scholars with a poetic touch have hoped so) another on the book of Job.[11]

He was never a match for the genius and influence of Augustine. A Briton by birth, his heresy is the one piece of theology that island gave the early Church. His scholarship was neither vast nor penetrating. But his piety is beyond dispute, his devotion both to good sense and the Gospels apparent, and his ideas have persevered, not only in the writings of the Semipelagians within the later Church but in many products of the Romantic movement.

The Pelagian heresy is best described in Augustine's refutation of it:

Universa igitur massa poenas debet et, si omnibus debitum damnationis supplicium redderetur, non iniuste procul dubio redderetur. Qui ergo inde per gratiam liberantur, non vasa meritorum suorum, sed vasa misericordiae nominantur. Cuius misericordiae nisi illius, qui Christum Iesum misit in hunc mundum peccatores salvos facere, quos praescivit et praedestinavit et vocavit et iustificavit et glorificavit? quis igitur usque adeo dementissime insaniat ut non agat ineffabiles gratias misericordiae quos voluit liberantis, qui recte nullo modo posset culpare iustitiam universos omnino damnantis?

.   .   .   .   .   .   .   .   .   .   .

Hoc si secundum scripturas sapiamus, non cogimur contra christianam gratiam disputare et ea dicere,

quibus demonstrare conemur naturam humanam neque
in parvulis medico indigere, quia sana est, et in maiori-
bus sibi ipsam ad iustitiam, si velit, posse sufficere.
Acute quippe videntur haec dici, sed in sapientia verbi,
qua evacuatur crux Christi, "non est ista sapientia
desursum descendens."

The whole human race, therefore, is bound to punishment, and if the agony of damnation is inflicted on
those who owe this debt, certainly it is not inflicted
unjustly. So those who have been freed of their debt by
grace are not vessels filled with their own virtues, but
vessels full of forgiveness. And whose forgiveness is
this, if not his who sent Christ Jesus into the world to
save sinners, whom he foreknows and foredestines,
calling them to justification and glory? Who could be
so totally mad as not to credit the inexpressible actions
of grace to the mercy of God who frees whom he
pleases, especially as God's justice cannot in any way
be blamed for man's universal damnation?

.   .   .   .   .   .   .   .   .   .   .   .

Rightly understanding the scriptures on this point,
we can no longer argue against the grace of Christ nor
hope to prove that the human nature of children needs
no doctor because of its health or that adults are
sufficient of themselves, if they wish to be, to find
justification. Those who say these things say them with
the devious wisdom which reduces Christ's Cross to
nothing. "This wisdom descendeth not from above."
(James 3:15)[12]

Pelagius had asserted that man was endowed with
sufficient grace from birth to lead a perfect life, if he
could; that Adam's sin was not binding on his posterity.
His theory of the perfectibility of mankind, in which
Plato's myth of the perfectible soul from the *Timaeus*
seems to be present, met with Augustine's firm opposition,
an opposition developed not so much in response to

Pelagius as out of his own experience, interpretation of scripture (which in one crucial instance was mislead by a faulty translation), and his insight into the metaphysical needs of the Church. Although Pelagius appeared on the scene long after Augustine's own thinking on the subjects at issue had begun to crystallize, he embodied the main challenge to the Augustinian thesis.

In denying Original Sin as Augustine conceived it, Pelagius was well within the traditions of the early Church as well as those of Greek philosophy. In the *Phaedrus*, Plato had proposed a notion of a fall in which the winged soul descends into the realm of matter, not because of willful sin, but because "καί τινι συντυχίᾳ χρησαμένη λήθης τε καὶ κακίας πλησθεῖσα βαρυνθῇ," "through some accident [the soul] is overcome with forgetfulness and evil and grows heavy."[13] The key word is "συντυχίᾳ," "accident," a completely neutral word devoid of moral implications. Plato's fall is not a moral one, but a failure correctly to perceive and remember Reality, and this failure can, in the transmutations of time, be overcome by the soul's acting alone and utilizing "ψυχῆς κυβερνήτη . . . νῷ," "reason, the soul's pilot."[14] Augustine fundamentally changed this conception of the Fall by making it moral, religious, and dependent on the individual will, where Plato and Pelagius had made it ontological, philosophical, and dependent on a general and abstract principle.

The early Fathers of the Church did not go far beyond Plato in their conception of the Fall. Once Irenaeus had established that all men are the debtors of God, "quem in primo quidem Adam offendimus," "whom we first offended in Adam," he went no further.[15] The Fall had been a universal calamity from which all still suffered but for which no one now living might really be said to be responsible. This notion is at once philosophical, in that it requires no religious apparatus such as baptism to deal with the fallen state (Irenaeus believed in baptism, but not because of any Original Sin),[16] and Pelagian, in that it absolves the individual will of corruption—Adam's sin is a transgression, but our sin is, for us, an accidental result of his.

Origen likewise holds a philosophical idea of the pervasiveness of sin which maintains that the Fall occurred before time began;[17] again, when we are born, sin is something that has already happened to us, not something which we have caused. We are born into a world of sin, but our wills are not directly involved in that sin. Perhaps Tertullian, who dwelt on the way in which sin was transmitted through the flesh, from generation to generation, through intercourse, comes closest to the Augustinian mark, but here too, the sin with which the child is born is accidental; the child is not its perpetrator, but its victim, and this happenstantial nature of sin explains why Tertullian discouraged child baptism. In fact, when he speaks of children, Tertullian, who in many ways is nearest Augustine of the early Fathers, sounds distinctly like a Pelagian:

> Ait quidem dominus, "nolite illos prohibere ad me venire." Veniant ergo dum adolescunt, veniant dum discunt, dum quo veniant docentur; fiant Christiani cum Christum nosse potuerint: quid festinat innocens aetas ad remissionem peccatorum?

> The Lord has said, "Suffer the children to come unto me." Let them come, then, when they are grown to

adolescence; let them come while they learn, while
they are taught where they are going. Let them become
Christians when they are able to know Christ. Why rush
the innocence of youth to the remission of sins?[18]

When the lines of battle between Pelagius and Augustine
were drawn, the tradition of the early Church seemed to
favor Pelagius.

It was this tradition, in the person of Pelagius, that
Augustine fought. If men were in fact free to stand or fall
of their own volition, not only was Christ's sacrifice ludicrous, but the authority of the Church as well. Given the
doctrine of Original Sin, however, Christ's death and
Resurrection are pertinent to all men at all times, and the
authority of the Church is secure through its adminis-
tration of the sacrament of baptism, by which Original
Sin is remitted.

Nor is this sacrament to be reserved for adults only,
for allowing the proposition that men must come to baptism by a rational act of choice is tantamount to denying
the mysterious (we might say the psychological) aspect of
Christianity. If, as Pelagius maintained, "we are born as
well without virtue as without vice and before the activity
of our own personal will there is nothing in man but
what God has stored in him,"[19] then Christianity must
become a rational philosophy, an adjunct of Platonism,
dependent for its validity on the wisdom and reason of
those who turn to it in maturity. Original Sin eliminates
this difficulty, asserts the mysterious element not only of
Christ's redemption but of the inherent sin within us,
and makes of Christianity a universal, mystical religion
in opposition to the rational philosophies of the pagan
world.

As a matter of course, infant baptism became a central issue in the Pelagian controversy. The practice had the sanction of popular tradition behind it, since from the first century laymen sometimes had had their children baptized before their first birthday. But as mentioned, Tertullian was opposed to the practice, and as late as Gregory of Nyssa Church thinkers seem to have considered baptism the act of adult, rational minds.[20] Augustine reversed this tradition of the early Church, made infant baptism a central feature of dogma, and in the process opened a whole new role for the child. By the time of the Council of Carthage in 416, at which a great deal of Augustine's thought passed into doctrine, infant baptism had been recognized as an essential feature of a universal and mystical religion: "If any one says that new-born children need not be baptized, or that they are baptized for the remission of sins, but that no Original Sin is derived from Adam to be washed away in the laver of regeneration, so that in their case the baptismal formula 'for the remission of sins' is to be taken in a fictitious and not in its true sense, let him be anathema."[21]

The Augustinian position and the refutation of the Pelagian heresy brought down upon the child the great weight of Christian dogma, making him a centerpiece where before, in the Greek and Roman cultures, he had been an object of neglect:

> What then was my sin? Was it that I hung upon the breast and cried . . . ? Or was it then good, even for a while, to cry for what, if given, would hurt? bitterly to resent, that persons free, and its own elders, yea, the very authors of its birth, served it not? that many besides, wiser than it, obeyed not the nod of its good

pleasure . . . ? The weakness then of infant limbs, not
its will, is its innocence. Myself have seen and known
even a baby envious.[22]

Autobiography and Original Sin enter the world together,
and the author of them both was St. Augustine. His experience, as shown here in the *Confessions,* laid the
groundwork for his doctrine, which gains much of its force
from the acute psychology manifested in this passage. In
the Augustinian view, the child is perhaps subrational, but
this is of small importance and properly the business of
philosophy, not religion. More important, the child is a
creature of will, a sinner *ab ovo,* and in this no different
from adults. Unbaptized, the child was consigned to the
flames of hell, an unpleasant but necessary conclusion of
the stated premises of Original Sin. Augustine himself had
difficulty tolerating the idea of damned infants, but he did
not relent.[23] In reaction to the damnation of the unbaptized, the Pelagians advanced the theory of *limbo,* a place
neither heaven nor hell, a void spot for innocent but unbaptized children. But the theory smacked too much of
rationalism and denial of binding sin, and the Council
of Carthage condemned it, though it speaks well for
the Church that the anathematizing canon was later
suppressed.[24]

So where the child had previously been ignored or
neglected in Western civilization, he was suddenly, at least
among the Fathers of the Church, of great moment. For
the Augustinians, the child became an adult figure, his
innocence a purely negative phenomenon residing in his
lack of bodily development but not in his lack of wilful-
ness. To the Pelagians, who had originally adopted the
classical posture regarding childhood, the Augustinian

position seemed both unreasonable and severe. Augustine's stress on the corruption of the will, even in childhood, removed reason from the supreme position it had held in the mainstream of Greek and Roman thought, and for the Pelagians, the clear light of reason, which illuminated their world with the same optimistic serenity Heraclitus had enjoyed a millennium earlier, was challenged and grew dim in the face of the new dogma. The Semipelagian concept of a *limbo puerorum* is a sentimental response to the rigors of the Original Sin argument, designed to relegate the thoughtless, unreasoning child to a neutral cosmological position similar to the station he had held in classical society and literature. And precisely because the limbo theory assumed the child to be without reason or will, strict Augustinian dogmatists eschewed it, although Aquinas argues for a *limbo puerorum* and Dante portrays the unlikely company of infants and the authors of antiquity, the latter presumably spared the extreme pains of hell by virtue of their abundant reason, the former by their total lack of it (*Inferno* 4.33–42).

Augustine's doctrine laid the foundation for the child as a literary image. He had connected childhood and sin, made the infant an adult of sorts, and surrounded him with a fallen nature, which existed in that condition because of man's fallen will. To this he added the concept of a second birth in baptism, a true and mysterious innocence as distinct from the seeming innocence of the child's weak limbs as the earthly city is from the city of God. The Pelagians and Semipelagians had argued for a primary innocence in the child, an innocence inherent in the flesh, and this argument in turn generated the sentimental notion of a limbo.

Centuries passed before the Church and its members could digest Augustinianism on a symbolic level—or even a dogmatic one. Pelagian theories reappeared throughout the Middle Ages to trouble the dogma of Original Sin, and not until the Council of Trent was the issue finally resolved in the Latin church.[25] Meanwhile the classical silence and neglect of childhood prevailed in literature as it almost certainly did in life.[26] Not until the Reformation, which itself might be viewed as a symptom that the dogmatic developments of the early Church had finally been accepted by the mass of the faithful not simply as belief but as metaphor and symbolism, does the child emerge as a literary figure around whom ideas of our original nature, our fallen condition, and our hopes for salvation cluster.

# II

# The Preromantic English Tradition

There are, of course, exceptions to the silence surrounding children during the period from Augustine to the Reformation. The temptation is to mention the least attractive of these first, the young martyr of Chaucer's Prioress's Tale. From the brevity and bigotry of the tale, it seems Chaucer purposely turned the Prioress's sentimentality over the innocence of the child against her, as well as denigrating her by putting into her mouth a subject thought unfit for artistic representation—the story of a child.

But while Chaucer used the child as a weapon against the Prioress, to the north the *Pearl* poet invested the infant with its full Augustinian solemnity to give English its first true child figure:

> Thou lyfed not two yer in oure thede;
> Thou cowthes never God nauther plese n pray,
> Ne never nawther Pater ne Crede
> And quen mad on the fyrst day![1]

says the *Pearl* dreamer in a fit of pique that a two-year-old child, simply by virtue of baptism, should be accorded the glories attendant upon the completion of a full, adult Christian life. Indeed, one of the functions of *Pearl* is to correct this Pelagian complaint made by the dreamer of the poem.

The young girl of the poem, who died in infancy, is at once a child, a pearl, and a maiden—or rather three aspects of one phenomenon, an innocence possible to all Christians. Baptized childhood is a kind of priceless adulthood, and so the child is transformed into a maiden without difficulty, since the infant's will is like that of an adult's. But the maiden is also the pearl of the poem:

> Jesus con call to hym his mylde,
> And sayde hys ryche no wyy myght wynne
> Bot he com thyder ryght as a chylde,
> Or elles nevermore com therinne.
> Harmles, trwe, and undefylde,
> Withouten mote other mascle of sulpande synne—
> Quen such ther cnoken on the bylde,
> Tyt schal hem men the yate unpynne.
> Ther is the blys that con not blynne
> That the jueler soghte thurgh perre pres,
> And solde alle hys goud, bothe wolen and lynne,
> To bye hym a perle was mascelles.     (721–732)

Childhood is at once a state on a par with adulthood and one of spotless innocence (provided of course that the child has been baptized, as the poem makes very clear).[2] The combination of these two ideas comes very close to being a definition of heaven on earth, and it is this state of adult perfection, represented by the dead, innocent child, toward which the dreamer strives. The poem's later visions of the heavenly city adorned with pearls are vistas of human and earthly possibilities: "But ay wolde man of happe more hente" (1195), the dreamer laments, and he awakens in the garden where his pearl was lost, which is by inference the same garden in which Adam forfeited the possibility of his innocent adulthood.

The *Pearl* poet brings the figure of the child a long way

from Horace's Lalage, though it is important to note that in both cases the child is a young girl. In later poetry, when the sexual allusion surrounding Lalage was combined with doctrinal significance on the order of the *Pearl* infant, the result would be a highly evocative (or provocative) image, such as Marvell uses in "Young Love," "The Picture of Little T.C. in a Prospect of Flowers," and *Upon Appleton House,* as well as later in a figure like Lewis Carroll's Alice. Of course, as the original debates and heresies which had brought the child into the lexicon of Christian thought and imagery receded in time, the direct connection between childhood and baptism was obscured, though authors such as Dickens and George Eliot continue to link the two. But the *Pearl* poet is careful to join the idea of sacrament and salvation explicitly.

By Spenser's time, the connection was still apparent if not as direct as in *Pearl*. In *The Faerie Queene* Ruddymane, the orphaned baby of Mordant and Amavia, is used in a context that still suggests baptism: his tiny hands are stained with the guilty blood of his parents and cannot be washed clean in any natural fountain or stream. Sir Guyon

> wist not whether blot of foule offence
> Might not be purgd with water nor with bath;
> Or that high God, in lieu of innocence,
> Imprinted had that token of his wrath,
> To shew how sore bloudguiltinesse he hat'th.
>
> (2.2.4)

Spenser is still close to the doctrinal sources of the child image, and the link between childhood, baptism, and Original Sin is clear enough in this passage. But Spenser, like authors who follow him, is more interested in moving the child figure out of this specific context and toward a more general and more pliable imagery:

> Poore Orphane in the wide world cattered,
> As budding braunch rent from the native tree,
> And throwen forth, till it be withered:
> Such is the state of men: thus enter wee
> Into this life with woe, and end with miseree.
>
> (2.2.2)

The tripartite image of the *Pearl* infant, who is at once child, virgin, and pearl, is reduced to a unified concept in later meditational poetry:

> *That Prospect* was the Gate of Hev'n; *that Day*
> The ancient Light of Eden did convey
> Into my Soul: I was an *Adam* there,
>     A little *Adam* in a Sphere
> Of joys; O there my ravisht Sense
> Was entertain'd in Paradise;
> And had a Sight of Innocence
> Which was to mee beyond all Price.
> An Antepast of Heven sure!
>     For I on Earth did reign:
> Within, without me, all was pure:
> I must becom a Child again.
>
> ("Innocence," 49–60)

In Traherne's as in Vaughan's childhood poems, childhood has become such a unified concept that it passes into the realm of abstraction. "An Infant-Ey," "The Return," both "Innocence" poems—wherever Traherne speaks of childhood, flesh and blood are gone from the idea. When he says "I must becom a Child again," it is impossible to picture him in his nursery. Clearly, he envisions a state of mind and soul and is not looking backward in time, but either forward or out of time altogether toward transcendence. While the connection with the doctrine of Original Sin is clearly drawn—it is the motive for using the child image in the first place—there is a purposeful paleness about the whole poem which is nicely captured by Vaughan's expression, "a white, Celestiall thought."

Vaughan's use of the childhood theme moves even more in the direction of the abstract. In the first lines of "The Retreate" quoted above, his is an "angell-infancy," and the sense of abstracting the angelic from the clay of mortality permeates his use of the child figure. For him, childhood is not a corporeal state at all, but a Neoplatonic condition of preexistence:

> O how I long to travell back
> And tread again that ancient track!
> That I might once more reach that plaine,
> Where first I left my glorious traine.
>
> (21–24)

The paleness of the childhood image in Traherne and Vaughan seems a necessary counterpart of their meditational and metaphysical goals. Having carried Augustine's thought to extremes almost Manichaean, they chose to bleach out the realistic aspect of childhood and dwell exclusively on its symbolic value.

Marvell, in contrast to the meditational poets, is the poet of green. Without sacrificing any of Vaughan's or Traherne's metaphysical goals, Marvell is able to present his child figures with a realism and a sense of humor akin to Lewis Carroll's presentation of Alice. In his work on Marvell's poetry, J. B. Leishman gives a detailed history of the appearance of young girls in earlier seventeenth-century poetry (the Cavaliers drew on Horace, the Puritans on Augustine). Marvell's children have the mystical aspect of the meditational child, the undeveloped sexual facet of Horace's Lalage, and the earthy possibilities of Christian redemption found in the *Pearl* image, as well as vivid life. Of the three children Marvell addresses, two are young girls whom he knew, Theophilia Cornewall of "T.C." and Mary Fairfax of *Upon Appleton House*. Yet despite the fact the children are taken from life, they are treated in such similar ways that they form a single image with two important facets characteristic of the child figure—their reflective function and their peculiar agility with language and naming.

The reflective capacity of the child is easily illustrated by jumping forward from Marvell to another poet like him in many ways—Hopkins. His "Spring and Fall: To a Young Child" offers in a few lines the basis of the reflective function of the child:

> Margaret, are you grieving
> Over Goldengrove unleaving?
> .    .    .    .    .    .    .    .    .
> It is the blight man was born for,
> It is Margaret you mourn for.

The child's identification with fallen nature (the title of the piece makes the theme of the Fall explicit) is so close that her emotional response to the external world is in part remorse and penitence. In Marvell, there is the same identification of the child and the created universe, but at first glance the relationship seems marked by a Pelagian purity:

> 'Tis *She* that to these Gardens gave
> That wondrous Beauty which they have;
> *She* streightness on the Woods bestows;

> To *Her* the Meadow sweetness owes;
> Nothing could make the River be
> So Chrystal-pure but only *She;*
> *She* yet more Pure, Sweet, Streight, and Fair,
> Then Gardens, Woods, Meads, Rivers are.
>
> (*Upon Appleton House*, 689–696)

Maria is the ideal type of nature, which reflects her so absolutely that "by her *Flames,* in *Heaven* try'd, / *Nature* is wholly vitrifi'd" (687–688). The entire creation is turned to glass by her power and consequently reflects her. As the type of the natural world, the child naturally holds vast sway over the created universe:

> Mean time, whilst every verdant thing
> It self does at thy Beauty charm,
> Reform the errours of the Spring.
>
> ("T.C.," 25–27)

Like Hopkins, Marvell makes nature and the child either symbiotic or identical. In this, both poets develop the child according to strict Augustinian doctrine, and it would seem they differ only as to whether the child—and the created world she represents—is originally fallen.

But the idea of the Fall is never far from Marvell's mind, and even his innocent children partake of it:

> But O young beauty of the Woods,
> Whom Nature courts with fruits and flow'rs,
> Gather the Flow'rs, but spare the Buds;
> Lest Flora angry at thy crime,
> To kill her Infants in their prime,
> Do quickly make th' Example Yours;
>       And, ere we see,
> Nip in the blossome all our hopes and Thee.
>
> ("T.C.," 33–40)

Here the idea of the Fall is introduced in a way that also draws on Horace. The Christian half of the sentiment in this stanza says that the child is the type of nature, which reflects her; therefore any alteration in nature is an alteration of self, and an evil alteration ("thy crime") will recoil on the innocent. But the evil alteration Marvell gives us is not from the Church but from Horace. The bud she might pick is not yet ready—*nondum*. The purpose of the bud, and presumably the child, is to come to maturity, a maturity which the imagery makes explicitly sexual. Such a conclusion naturally leads to a paradox: "all our hopes" depend on a future maturity, but this maturity is, in contrast to the pure innocence of the child, fallen and sexual; therefore, our redemption is to be achieved through corruption.

Instead of dissolving this paradox, Marvell simply allows it to stand (it is a paradox not unlike the one involved in the medieval notion of a *felix culpa,* a fortunate Fall of Man—a notion which Milton found extremely attractive). All Marvell hopes to do with this paradox is change the tone of it. Our hopes of attaining the childhood state of innocence depend upon our own maturity, both spiritual and physical, for if the world is to come to this happy state, procreation is a necessity. Maturity is a step we are obliged to take on the path to innocence. The poet, writing from a mature (the dogmatist will say corrupt) distance, seems to treat the child with a respectful admiration which barely disguises reproof. T.C. is "this virtuous Enemy of Man" (16) and Maria is a grave creature with "judicious eyes" (653) from whom the poet hides his writing instruments in *Upon Appleton House.* It might have given Marvell a melancholy sort of pleasure that the mature Mary Fairfax married George Villiers, second Duke of Buckingham, of whom Dryden wrote that he was "Stiff in opinions, always in the wrong; / Was everything by starts, and nothing long" (*Absalom and Achitophel*, 547–548); his pupil was abundantly present in the world of mature corruption through which the path to redeemed innocence lies.

The other function of the child in these two poems by Marvell is its naming or linguistic capacity:

> In the green Grass she loves to lie,
> And there with her fair Aspect tames
> The Wilder flow'rs, and gives them names;
>
> ("T.C.," 3–5)
>
> For *She,* to higher Beauties rais'd,
> Disdains to be for lesser prais'd.
> *She* counts her Beauty to converse
> In all the Languages as *hers;*
> Nor yet in those *her self* imployes
> But for the *Wisdome,* not the *Noyse;*
> Nor yet that *Wisdome* would affect,
> But as 'tis *Heavens Dialect.*
>
> (*Upon Appleton House,* 705–712)

In the Platonic myth from the *Timaeus* quoted above, the naming capacity is the property of the soul as it reaches rationality, but in the Christian myth, it is Adam's function, here arrogated to the child. Nor is it unusual to find the child figure assuming the functions of Adam. Increasingly, children became the realistic counterpart of the mythic Eden couple. As a real-life Adam, the child inherits his power to speak the prelapsarian tongue all men spoke before Babel (Babel is probably meant in Marvell's line, "But for the *Wisdome,* not the *Noyse*").

For Milton, Hebrew was the language of the Garden, but for an age adapting myth to realism, the language of Paradise was the language of children. Blake makes great use of the idea, but it is present here in Marvell. From these associations with Eden the child image acquired its "wise child" dimension, as well as a certain cuteness and cleverness which we attribute to Eve and from which we trace the Fall.

Marvell's use of the child figure illustrates the larger flux of imagery in an age which produced the philosophy of Locke and the critical theory of Dryden: just as the age sought to make wit and judgment a single phenomenon and strove to eliminate the troubling distinction between words and things, so that one would replicate the other, in their imagery the Augustans tried to combine the mythic and the matter-of-fact. The figures of *The Dunciad* are both actual individuals of eighteenth-century English society and mythic creations who exist in epic time and space. This dualism works on the same principle as the heroic couplet: the two halves are painfully distinct, but taken together, give a third sense which, without infringing on either of its parts, almost seems like a third member subliminally inserted in the couplet form. Children lent themselves handsomely to this type of image-making; their matter-of-factness had been, from antiquity, established through indifference, yet Christian dogma gave to them mythic overtones of Eden, of the Fall, of man's free will and salvation. Gray's "Ode on a Distant Prospect of Eton College" (1742) demonstrates the way in which the Augustans developed the actual and the mythic aspects of the child in a single image, which, in form if not substance, was bequeathed to the romantics, the Victorians, and our own era.

In Marvell's poems on youth the poet sets himself at a remove from the child which gives his wit and perception a freedom not to be found in the meditational poets, while at the same time emphasizing the distance between the fallen artist and his paradisical subject. In Gray this distance is raised to the level of a conceit. "Distant" is not only the key word of the title, but an idea carefully nourished throughout the first stanza and the poem as a whole:

> Ye distant spires, ye antique towers
> That crown the watry glade,
> Where grateful Science still adores
> Her HENRY's holy Shade;
> And ye, that from the stately brow
> Of WINDSOR's heights th' expanse below
> Of grove, of lawn, of mead survey,
> Whose turf, whose shade, whose flowers among
> Wanders the hoary Thames along
> His silver-winding way.           (1–10)

There are numerous distances here—the physical distance of the poet from what he observes (which is a theme of the "Elegy" as well), the historical distance of present from past, the distance of court and convention from natural simplicity (reflected even in the capitalization), and behind the rest, the distance of the writer from himself, which is the distance between childhood and maturity, between Eton and the prospect overlooking it, and between Eden and our world.

The poem revolves around this sense of distance, using the child figure as its focal point:

> Ah happy hills, ah pleasing shade,
> Ah fields belov'd in vain,
> Where once my careless childhood stray'd,
> A stranger yet to pain!

I feel the gales, that from ye blow,
A momentary bliss bestow,
As waving fresh their gladsome wing,
My weary soul they seem to soothe,
And, redolent of joy and youth,
To breathe a second spring.    (11–20)

Gray is in many ways the poetic disciple of Locke (he
undertook a Latin poem, *De principiis cogitandi,* in order
to do for Locke's philosophy of the understanding what
Lucretius had done for Epicurus), and part of the sense
of distance in the "Ode" can be traced to an empirical
impulse to achieve understanding through what Locke
called the "art and pains" of a distant perspective: "The
understanding, like the eye, whilst it makes us see and
perceive all other things, takes no notice of itself; and it
requires art and pains to set it at a distance and make it
its own object."[3]

In Gray, however, the "art and pains" are not seen
simply in the context of attaining a higher wisdom. They
become the melancholy torment which is the penalty paid
by man for civilization. In the "Ode," the understanding
makes the adult conscious that he is civilized, and to be
civilized is to be doomed:

Alas, regardless of their doom,
The little victims play!
No sense have they of ills to come,
Nor care beyond to-day:
Yet see how all around 'em wait
The Ministers of human fate,
And black Misfortune's baleful train!
Ah, shew them where in ambush stand
To seize their prey the murth'rous band!
Ah, tell them, they are men!    (51–60)

Throughout the Eton "Ode" adulthood is used as a metaphor of the "baleful," fallen condition of civilization; it is a doomed state. Childhood, on the other hand, becomes a vehicle for investigating the original condition of society and ascertaining the fundamentals of man's role within civilization. The young Etonians, traditionally the future pillars of English society and civilization, make the image of childhood in the "Ode" even more pointedly about the relationship between "doom," civilized life, and the original state which necessitates them both.

Gray uses the child figure to express his belief that the rational state of adulthood is not only the highest evolution of the human species, as Locke would have it, but a condition in which man must be painfully conscious of his fallen nature. In this sense, children are "little victims"; their understanding is still undeveloped, and hence, like Aristotle's children, they cannot fully participate in the benefits of civilization. But at the same time, Gray's children are spared the terrifying consciousness of the world's doomed state and their own. The child is caught in a paradox: to be a man, he must accept this painful knowledge, while to try to remain a child is to fail to meet one's human potential. Some of Gray's Etonians, "bold adventurers," are aware of living inside this paradox, and for them it produces "a fearful joy" as they live out their childhood:

> While some on earnest business bent
> Their murm'ring labours ply
> 'Gainst graver hours, that bring constraint
> To sweeten liberty:
> Some bold adventurers disdain
> The limits of their little reign,

And unknown regions dare descry:
Still as they run they look behind,
They hear a voice in every wind,
And snatch a fearful joy.          (31–40)

The first four lines of the stanza give us the picture of youth aiming at adulthood, "graver hours" whose liberty is constraint filled with "earnest business" and "labours." Then three lines give us the "bold adventurers," who are conscious of an "unknown region." The final three lines give us the conflict inevitable when the first two ideas are brought together, finely expressed in the oxymoron, "a fearful joy."

If anyone doubts that Gray's emotions are all ranged on the side of childhood as he has pictured it, the next stanza eliminates the doubt:

Gay hope is theirs by fancy fed,
Less pleasing when possest;
The tear forgot as soon as shed,
The sunshine of the breast:
Theirs buxom health of rosy hue,
Wild wit, invention ever-new,
And lively chear of vigour born;
The thoughtless day, the easy night,
The spirits pure, the slumbers light,
That fly th' approach of morn.

(41–50)

Throughout the "Ode," Gray is suspended between an exuberant romanticism (this last stanza, by itself, might have come directly from Wordsworth) and a careful, melancholy empiricism derived from Locke.

With Locke, Gray rejects Innate Ideas. The Etonians are

"thoughtless"; their minds are *tabulae rasae* awaiting the imprint of understanding, which the poet at his remove already possesses. But in neither Gray nor Locke does the rejection of Innate Ideas imply a rejection of all things innate, which in effect would have been to reject the concept of Original Sin on which so much Christian—and especially Protestant—dogma rests. In the *Essay* Locke says: "Nature, I confess, has put into man a desire of happiness and an aversion to misery: these indeed are innate practical principles which (as practical principles ought) *do* continue constantly to operate and influence all our actions without ceasing: these may be observed in all persons and all ages, steady and universal; but these are *inclinations of the appetite* to good, not impressions of truth on the understanding. I deny not that there are natural tendencies imprinted on the minds of men."[4] But where Locke regarded these "inclinations of the appetite" as an animal function unworthy of detailed discussion and placed understanding in the forefront of his philosophy as that which "sets man above the rest of sensible beings, and gives him all the advantages and dominion which he has over them,"[5] Gray found both beauty and importance in thoughtless appetite. The "gay hope," "the tear forgot as soon as shed," the "buxom health of rosy hue"—these are for Gray pleasures which are an end in themselves and which represent an important counterbalance to "the Ministers of human fate" attendant on adulthood. Further, for Gray the appetite not only predates the understanding but also overwhelms it. The last stanza of the "Ode" sets out something very much like the romantic idea of natural joy, but is unable to find any transcendence in the concept:

To each his suff'rings: all are men,
Condemn'd alike to groan,
The tender for another's pain;
Th' unfeeling for his own.
Yet ah! why should they know their fate?
Since sorrow never comes too late,
And happiness too swiftly flies.
Thought would destroy their paradise.
No more; where ignorance is bliss,
'Tis folly to be wise.          (91–100)

The Augustan sense of life's folly pervades these lines, but the Augustans looked to Locke and understanding to save them as another age had looked to grace. Gray had no part of this: "Thought would destroy their paradise"; "ignorance is bliss." And yet he was still no romantic. What separates Gray from the romantics and gives his poetry its particular poignancy is his feeling that adulthood is an inevitable though unwelcome condition and that nature is a painful place in which men are not only outcasts from Paradise but possess no means of transcendence within fallen nature. Childhood is for Gray a medium through which the poet can look to gain perspective on man's fallen place in a fallen world and gauge the extent of the corruption in which he is involved. Moreover, this corruption comes with the development of that faculty which Locke had considered as the means of rational happiness, the understanding.

Gray himself prefixed the "Ode" with a particularly melancholy line from Menander which highlights his attitude in the poem: "Ἄνθρωπος, ἱκανὴ πρόφασις εἰς τὸ δυστυχεῖν," "I am a man; sufficient reason to be miserable."[6] But Menander spoke of being *human,* whereas Gray uses the line to mean, "I am an *adult;* sufficient reason to be miserable." By contrast, the child figure in Gray represents the human happiness possible before the understanding develops, bringing with it the unhappy organization of humanity into civilization. Horace Walpole, a kindred spirit and fellow preromantic, jotted a singularly apt line from Lucan in the margin of his copy of the "Ode": "Nec licuit populis parvum te, Nile, videre," "Nor have the people been allowed to see you when small, O Nile." [7] The inscription is a tribute to Gray's achievement in taking the image of childhood and examining it in a distant but feeling mode which incorporates a later realism, a romantic sensibility, and a vision of Paradise lost.

*Tristram Shandy* follows Gray's "Ode" by eighteen years, and like it, is generally considered a work of Lockean orthodoxy, virtually to the exclusion of good Christian dogma; *Tristram Shandy* is indeed built upon the principles of the association of ideas established by Locke, just as Gray's "Ode" is poised on Locke's conception of the understanding. But Gray does not swallow Locke whole; he rather takes his premises and builds upon them a structure quite different in realization from the work of the master. Such is Sterne's case as well in *Tristram Shandy*.

If *Tristram Shandy* is structured upon Locke's association of ideas, the purpose of that structure is not to demonstrate the reasonable capacity of mankind, but to adopt Locke to a Christian conception of fallen humanity.

*Tristram Shandy* is preeminently a lapsarian expedition, and it is altogether appropriate that its actions, both mental and physical, should be played out against the repeated images of the birth of the child figure. Indeed, the first sentence of the book, while acknowledging Locke ("not only the production of a rational Being was concerned in it"), immediately fixes the whole system of Locke's philosophy in the traditional framework of Christian doctrine:

> I wish either my father or my mother, or indeed both of them, as they were in duty both equally bound to it, had minded what they were about when they begot me; had they duly considered how much depended upon what they were then doing;—that not only the production of a rational Being was concerned in it, but that possibly the happy formation and temperature of his body, perhaps his genius and the very cast of his mind;—and, for aught they knew to the contrary, even the fortunes of his whole house might take their turn from the humours and dispositions which were then uppermost;—Had they duly weighed and considered all this, and proceeded accordingly,—I am verily persuaded I should have made a quite different figure in the world, from that, in which the reader is likely to see me.

The rational being is foremost a creature of the flesh, and the flesh, say Tristram and Sterne, ought to be under the restraints of duty. To reinforce the point that flesh has primacy over intellect, chapter 2 launches upon a digression concerning the homunculus, in which the spermatazoon is given equal standing with the completely reasonable man as "a Being of as much activity,—and, in all senses of the word, as much and as truly our fellow-creature as my Lord Chancellor of England." Here is Augustine gone one better! not only the infant in the crib, but the sperm itself is to be treated as adult. Or is this mere parody of Augustine?

Many readers of Sterne in his own day and thereafter have found in him parody alone and have held that he slighted the doctrines of the church in which he served. ("Do for shame, Mr. Shandy, hide your jerkin, or at least, send the lining to the scowerer's,"[8] said the *Monthly Review* on the publication of volumes 2 and 3 of *Tristram Shandy*.) To such critics Sterne replied in an epigram added to the frontispiece of the second edition of the fifth volume of *Tristram Shandy* (1762): "Si quis Clericus, aut Monachus, verba joculatoria, risum moventia sciebat, anathema esto," "If any priest or monk knows jesting words which incite laughter, let him be anathema." The formula is taken (apparently in distorted form)[9] from the proceedings of the Council of Carthage, the same council which made Augustine's view of Original Sin dogma. But is not the epigram itself a parody? Perhaps recourse to the sermons, which Dr. Johnson found so unworthy, can help to establish Sterne's orthodoxy, especially as regards the Christian idea of the Fall. Sterne's sermon, "Job's Account of the Shortness and Troubles of Life, Considered," is prefaced by Job's reflection, "Man that is born of a woman, is of few days, and full of trouble." It concludes in terms which completely support the orthodox view of the Fall:

> So that upon the whole, when we have examined the true state and condition of life, and have made some allowances for a few fugacious, deceitful pleasures, there is scarce anything to be found which contradicts Job's description of it—Whichever way we look abroad, we see some legible characters of what God first denounced

against us, "That in sorrow we should eat our bread, till we return to the ground from whence we were taken."

But some will say, Why are we thus to be put out of love with human life? To what purpose is it to expose the dark sides of it to us, or enlarge upon the infirmities which are natural, and consequently out of our power to redress?

I answer that the subject is nevertheless of great importance, since it is necessary every creature should understand his present state and condition to put him in mind of behaving suitably to it.—Does not an impartial survey of man—the holding up of this glass to show him his defects and natural infirmities, naturally tend to cure his pride, and clothe him with humility, which is a dress that best becomes a short-lived and a wretched creature?[10]

This melancholy assessment of life is fundamental to *Tristram Shandy;* life begins in misunderstanding, disfigurement, confusion, pain, quarrels, and separation of each creature from every other. It is, like the design of the book, imperfect and by definition unfinished (the book is built upon the imperfect, the unfinished sentence, the aposiopesis). And the image by which *Tristram Shandy* reinforces these opinions is the repeated recurrence to Tristram's birth. The child figure is kept ever-present, as a continual reminder that the absurdity and pain of childbirth (and here the text of Job which Sterne uses as the point of departure for the sermon above suggests itself) is an omnipresent condition of life itself.

Like Job, Sterne sees life beginning in sorrows, and with Gray (but against Locke) he views the coming of reason not as a means of redeeming man from the primordial folly, but of compounding it. It is the reasonable, Lockean

Tristram whose book deviates from the "straight paths" of Hebrews 12:3 into the convolutions of the existing novel: "What a journey!" (6.40); nothing could be more fitting than that *Tristram Shandy* should, as a piece of literature, be a model of what it describes: an incomplete, unreasonable work constantly in the act of being born.

Even the attack upon the doctors of the Sorbonne (1.20) for their defense of baptism of the unborn is a parody not so much of Romanism as it is of reasonable argument; the digression on baptism keeps the emerging infant and its salvation before the reader in theological, if parodic, terms, and here Sterne is Catholic enough to appeal in a footnote, from the Doctors to Aquinas, who held that "Infantes in maternis uteris existentes baptizari possunt *nullo modo*," "Children in the womb cannot be baptized *by any means*."

Here in the debate over baptism of the unborn, and earlier in the digression on the homunculus, the apparent satire achieves a threefold effect: first, and most obviously, it makes a mockery of the reason and logic which, if carried to their extremes, would have the spermatazoon baptized *in testes* (1.20); second, it keeps the issues apparently mocked vividly and controversially before the reader, thus, in one form, sustaining the very doctrines seemingly under attack; and third, through the form of satire itself, whose nature is to expose weakness, the digressions on infant baptism and the homunculus place even the reasonable development of a doctrine of Original Sin under the strictures of its own creation: the doctrine which maintains our corruption is, because of reasonable manufacture, corrupted itself. We are caught in an infinite regression of fallibility and imperfection, mirrored in all moments of human creation, and hence the child, as Augustine would have it, presides over all.

With Augustine, however, Sterne is a believer in grace, and the manifestation of that grace in *Tristram Shandy* is laughter. The satire of the fallen world is at once a recognition of our present state and a means of surmounting it in the wisdom and objectivity (Sterne might say, as he suggests in his sermon above, the humility) of humor; and, of course, it is Sterne's sense of humor which sustains the novel and remains with the reader.

Like Sterne's sense of satire and cerebral comedy, Fielding's robust and good-natured English humor has beguiled critics into reading his work as Pelagian,[11] and at first glance, *Tom Jones* (1754) is a work which promulgates the fitness of mankind and the potential for moral perfection latent in the human world. The bastard child recovers from and overcomes all stigma of his birth—in fact, he might be said to triumph over the doctrine of Original Sin entirely, laying waste to it as surely as he supplants Mr. Blifel.

But Fielding is too complex to be a mere Pelagian. There is in his conception of young Tom Jones and his portrait of humanity a deference to natural and inherent moral qualities (both good and ill) to which Pelagius would not have subscribed but which Calvin might have underwritten:

> For that immense variety of characters, so apparent in men even of the same climate, religion, and education . . . could hardly exist, unless the distinction had some original foundation in nature itself. . . .
> This original difference will, I think, alone account for that very early and strong inclination to good or evil,

which distinguishes different dispositions in children, in their first infancy; in the most uninformed savages, who can have thought to have altered their nature by no rules, nor artfully acquired habits; and lastly, in persons, who, from the same education, &c., might be thought to have directed nature the same way; yet, among all these, there subsists, as I have before hinted, so manifest and extreme a difference of inclination or character, that almost obliges us, I think, to acknowledge some unacquired, original distinction, in the nature or soul of one man, from that of another.

Thus, without asserting, in general, that man is a deceitful animal; we may, I believe, appeal for instances of deceit to the behaviour of some children and savages.[12]

Fielding has moved a step away from Original Sin—not all men are born evil in will—yet he affirms some disposition in nature which makes men either good or bad, and this is reminiscent of Calvin's theory of election. Young Tom Jones is, of course, one of the elect: Fielding as creator has ordained that no matter what befalls him, he shall survive and flourish. So in the treatment of Tom Jones, Fielding is a curious mixture of Pelagius and Calvin, at once looking back to the seventeenth century and forward to the heresies of Wordsworth.

But Fielding is something more in his treatment of the child: he is, in this regard at least, that rarity, a true neoclassicist; for with the ancients, he is not delighted by the depiction of childhood, and he is only too pleased to move, in two paragraphs, over the infancy of Tom Jones into the era of his budding reason and blooming sexuality; in fact, though the infant Jones has already been portrayed, Fielding speaks as if the reader could only really meet him not as a child, but as an adolescent:

It is a more useful capacity to be able to foretell the
actions of men in any circumstances from their characters than to judge of their characters from their actions.
The former, I own, requires the greater penetration,
but may be accomplished by true sagacity with no less
certainty than the latter.

As we are sensible that much the greater part of our
readers are very eminently possessed of this quality, we
have left them a space of twelve years to exert it in, and
shall now bring forth our hero at about fourteen years
of age, not questioning that many have been long im-
patient to be introduced to his acquaintance.     (3.1)

Perhaps Fielding, who mixes classicism, Pelagianism,
and Calvinism in equal parts, provides a fitting place to
halt and examine some of the premises of this study before
embarking on an examination of the child figure in the
romantic and postromantic periods.

The first premise, of course, is that children are figurative, at least as they appear in English literature over the
past 300 years. A beautiful and alluring woman in a book
or movie who is pictured eating an apple can be identified as
a figure or representation of Eve so quickly that the figure
may be rejected as hackneyed or stale. But the reader or
viewer, coming across a child, will be tempted to say,
"Well, here is something from real life, not a figure, but
just what it seems to be—a child." The fact that the child
is not regarded as a figure or image gives it added potency,
for the truth is that this particular depiction of reality is
relatively new to English literature. The foregoing survey
points up the lack of interest in the literary representation
of childhood demonstrated by the ancient world and
shows that the child first becomes prominent in the development and controversies of the early Church, es-

pecially in the debate over the question of Original Sin. When the child figure began to appear with more frequency in the seventeenth century, it owed its thematic conception and significance to these early debates of the Church.

Between the time of Augustine and that of the *Pearl* poet, however, there are a thousand years which maintain the classical facade of indifference to childhood. To explain why the child figure appears a millennium after the dogma in which it has its roots requires another assumption, namely that a religious doctrine requires a substantial incubation period before it can translate itself into symbolism and imagery. In other words, the child's participation in the Fall and in man's salvation may have been understood as an idea by the Church of the fifth century, but a thousand years were required before this idea was felt as a part of the unconscious view of life from which literature draws its figures and symbols. Having made this assumption, it is then possible to observe the gradual evolution of the child figure as it begins to embody certain themes, such as the question of free will, innocence, and the means of salvation, which had previously been expressed mythically, allegorically, and through other conventional imagery. Such a figure is naturally suited to the needs of a developing realism, and the language is richer for having a new image.

A final assumption is that not only is the child figurative, but the reader or viewer instinctively understands its figurative nature. A modern audience, confronted by phenomena as divergent as Dickens's Tiny Tim and James's Miles in *The Turn of the Screw,* or even Shirley Temple and Baby LeRoi, brings to the idea of childhood certain inherent notions as to what is about to be discussed. In this way, the debates of the Council of Carthage over the original nature of man are kept alive in the modern world both in the children of Dickens's novels and the deeply Augustinian pronouncements of W. C. Fields on the topic of childhood.

# III

## The Sentimental Aspects of the Child Figure: Wordsworth as Heretic

The children of Shakespeare's plays are drawn with a flourish of sentiment more characteristic of the Victorian era than the period in which they were created. The most notable example of this sentimental treatment is the picture Shakespeare gives us of the young princes in *Richard III*, just before the assassin Forrest smothers them:

> "Thus, thus," quoth Forrest, "girdling one another
> Within their alabaster innocent arms:
> Their lips were four red roses on a stalk,
> Which in their summer beauty kiss'd each other.
> A book of prayers on their pillow lay;
> Which once," quoth Forrest, "almost changed my mind."
>
> (4.3.9–15)

The scene has its source in More's *History of King Richard III*, where the sentiment it evokes is turned to political purpose; Shakespeare uses the same material for dramatic advantage. His interest in the children themselves is slight, and his willingness to portray childhood realistically is slighter still: Mamillius of *The Winter's Tale* sounds more like Touchstone than an infant:

> *Mam.* What color are your eyebrows?
> *First Lady.* Blue, my lord.

> *Mam.* Nay, that's a mock: I have seen a lady's nose
> That has been blue, but not her eyebrows.
>
> (1.2.13–15)

Both More and Shakespeare were not as concerned with childhood itself as with the sentiment inherent in the representation of childhood, the one using this sentiment for partisan history, the other for melodramatic effect.

The little princes of *Richard III,* as well as the children of *Titus Andronicus,* are either murder victims or helpless participants in a grotesque spectacle of carnage and death. The presence of these innocents in Shakespeare's melodramas heightens the sense of pervasive degeneracy and collapse, which is the climate of both plays, by creating a purposely heavy-handed and sentimental contrast to the obtuse perversions of the central action. In providing this contrast, the children help lift these plays out of the realm of historical drama and onto a plain of cosmic malfunction. Shakespeare's child victims, by the pathos of their representation, point to a larger, Augustinian drama behind the historical drama. The sentiment of innocence that childhood evokes in Shakespeare is a felt response to the brutal condition of fallen man, and this sentiment is as strong as the fallen state against which it reacts is shown to be corrupt. Behind Shakespeare's children there is always the idea of death and the mortal taste that first brought death into the world:

> Golden lads and girls all must,
> As chimney-sweepers, come to dust.
>
> (*Cymbeline,* 4.2.262–263)

This chapter will examine the golden lads of Wordsworth as well as the chimney sweeps of Blake and nineteenth-

century England with a view toward understanding the
ideas which lie behind their presentation and the sentiment
they evoke.

Shakespeare's brand of sentiment elicits an emotional
response by demonstrating that the innocence of childhood is a short-lived phenomenon in an otherwise blighted
world. The same kind of sentiment lies behind Marvell's
T.C., Gray's Etonians, and the escapist image of infancy
in Vaughan and Traherne. In each case, the poet imagines
that a golden age has existed in the past and that mankind
is continually moving away from this idyllic period, just as
the individual continually moves further from his childhood on his way to death. The classical concept of an
age of gold succeeded by progressively baser cycles is very
much present in this type of sentiment, which can be
called "conservative" because in its purest form (illustrated here from Vaughan's "The Retreate") it distrusts
the present and longs for the redemptive past:

> O how I long to travell back
> And tread again that ancient track!
> That I might once more reach that plaine,
> Where first I left my glorious traine.
>
> .    .    .    .    .    .    .    .    .
>
> But (ah!) my soul with too much stay
> Is drunk, and staggers in the way.
> Some men a forward motion love,
> But I by backward steps would move.
>
> (21–24, 27–30)

In this conservative view, the best service of the future is
that it will eventually bring humanity to that state of
total dissolution necessary for the apocalyptic restoration
of the primal golden state. The sort of sentiment derived

from this view, and then applied to children, very frequently revolves around the death of a child, as in *Richard
III* or the work of Dickens, who was the master of this
kind of sentimentality; from the conservative point of
view, the death of a child is felicitous and tragic in equal
parts—tragic in that it underlines the corrupt nature of
things as they are, felicitous in that it prefigures the universal demise which precedes the restoration of the world's
own childhood.

This conservative sentimentality is in accord with the
Christian doctrine discussed in the last chapter from which
children in English literature originally derive their interest
and importance. It is firmly rooted in the dogma of
Original Sin and in the belief that God's grace is necessary
to restore the prelapsarian state in individuals, just as his
apocalyptic intervention is required to restore it in the
cosmos as a whole. But in the eighteenth century, the
idea of childhood—and the sentiment attached to the
idea—took on a new coloring.[1] The children of Wordsworth and Rousseau are substantially different creatures
from the children already discussed here, whose representation grew more or less linearly out of Augustinian
theology. The kind of sentiment the children of Wordsworth and Rousseau evoke is consequently of a different
order from the conservative type exemplified by Vaughan's
"Retreate."

This change in the perception of the child figure, while
culminating in the work of Rousseau and Wordsworth,
was at least latently present in the first humanist forays
against the Scholastic system of education. If Rousseau is
reacting against Locke when he says in *Emile* (1762), "Of
all man's faculties, Reason, which is a combination of the

rest, is developed last and with greatest difficulty," [2] then
Locke is equally reacting against Milton's theory that "the
end . . . of learning is to repair the ruins of our first parents
by regaining to know God aright, and out of that knowledge to love him." [3] Milton in turn ridiculed the university
curriculum in which he had been trained. Putting aside
the points of difference in humanist educational theory,
there remains an overall movement toward concern and
sympathy with children, in which Rousseau figures as the
foremost representative of the Pelagian position. Whatever
the points of disagreement between Milton, Locke,
Rousseau, and their schools, they are nonetheless at odds
over the same issue.

What that issue is, Rousseau himself states succinctly
in his *Emile:*

> Let us lay it down as an incontestable maxim that the
> first promptings of nature are always right. There is no
> original corruption in the human heart: there is not a
> single vice to be found there of which one could not
> say how and by what means it entered. The only passion
> natural to man is self-love (*amour de soi*) or egoism
> (*amour propre*) taken in an extended sense. This passion,
> considered in itself, that is as relative to the individual,
> is good and useful; and, as it has no necessary relation
> to anyone else, it is in its nature indifferent: it becomes
> good or bad only from the application which we make
> of it and the relations which we give it. Up to the
> appearance, therefore, of the faculty which regulates this
> self-love, that is of Reason, a child should do nothing
> that implies a relation to others, but only what is
> required by Nature; he will then do nothing wrong. [4]

Taken together with his assertion in *Julie* (1761) that
"there is no criminal whose tendencies, had they been

better directed, would not have produced great virtues,"[5] the Pelagian nature of Rousseau's image of childhood becomes clear. Augustine had listed as two of the cardinal tenets of the Pelagian heretics, first, that "new-born infants are in the same condition as Adam before the Fall," and second, "that a man can be without sin, if he choose."[6] These are the fundamental theses of Rousseau's philosophy.

Where Rousseau differs from the original Pelagians and approaches Augustinian dogma is in the importance he attaches to childhood. But for him, the child is important not because he is a living type of man's state in Eden before the fall, but because he represents—not figuratively but in flesh and blood—man's potential for immediate and future freedom and fulfillment: "He has not had most life who has lived most years, but he who has felt life the most. A man may be buried a hundred years old and have died in his cradle. Such a one would have gained by dying in youth if he had *lived* till then."[7] The sentiment which grows out of Rousseau's version of childhood is not based on a contrast between man's fallen nature and his original innocence or on the bittersweet expectation of universal dissolution. It is based on "the feeling of life." For Rousseau, the innocence usually associated with the lost Eden is available here and now. His sentiment looks through the present to the immediate future and can therefore be called "progressive." His golden age is not mythic but palpable, not reached by grace but by education of the individual will. The following passage from *Emile* demonstrates Rousseau's sentimental attitude to childhood and defines it as well:

When I picture to myself a boy of ten or twelve, healthy, strong and well built for his age, only pleasant thoughts arise in me, whether for his present or his future. I see him bright, eager, vigorous, carefree, completely absorbed in the present, rejoicing in abounding vitality. I see him in the years ahead using senses, mind and power as they develop from day to day. I view him as a child and he pleases me. I think of him as a man and he pleases me still more. His warm blood seems to heat my own. I feel as if I were living in his life and am rejuvenated by his vivacity.[8]

Something of this kind of sentiment, which in English literature is usually considered the domain of Wordsworth, was already apparent by the time of Ambrose ("Namby-Pamby") Philips. His "To Miss Charlotte Pulteney, in her mother's arms, May 1, 1724" may serve as an example of the kind of polite and pretty verse about children which had a certain vogue in the Augustan age:

> Simple maiden, void of art,
> Babbling out the very heart.
>
> (11–12)

But even Philips, whose pretty charms earned him the scorn and derision of his contemporaries, injects a curious, and very English, note into his childhood poems. The lines which follow those given above are

> Yet abandoned to thy will,
> Yet imagining no ill,
> Yet too innocent to blush,
> Like the linnet in the bush.
>
> (13–16)

The sense of foreboding conjured up by "yet," the coupling of "abandoned" and "will," and the juxtaposition of present innocence and future blush—all these conspire to return the poem's picture of childhood to the Augustinian tradition in which Philips's contemporary Isaac Watts was then writing:

> Great God, how terrible art thou
> To sinners e'er so young![9]

English poetry—even Wordsworth's—seems unable to render the whole of Rousseau's vision of childhood. The gloomy but perhaps more interesting and poetically rewarding notion of the child as a figure who owes his existence to Original Sin is present in even the most devout English followers of Rousseau. Thomas Day's *Sandford and Merton* (1783–1789) took *Emile* as its starting point and translated Rousseau's precepts into children's literature. It is the story of Harry Sandford and Tommy Merton, the first the son of "a plain honest farmer," the second, of a capitalist grown rich in the sugar trade. Harry, a child of nature and natural education, is the embodiment of Rousseau's vision of childhood. Tommy, on the other hand, is spoiled, timorous, and stuck-up. *Sandford and Merton* revolves around Tommy's conversion to, and confirmation in, the philosophy of natural piety through Tommy's friendship with Harry and their tutelage under Mr. Barlow, the local parson—who seems to have absorbed more Rousseau than gospel. In fact, Day himself wrote that if all the books in the world were to be destroyed, "the second book I should wish to save, after the Bible, would be Rousseau's *Emilius*."[10]

Even Day, however, the most unflinching English follower of Rousseau, is full of quirks and oddities that might have startled his French master. Tommy's spoiled character makes him very greedy at the table, with the unpleasant result that he is often cut by knives, bruised by collapsing serving-trays, or scalded by the tea things which impede his unnatural voracity. In another incident foreign to Rousseau's disciplined but benign concept of nature, Tommy and Harry test their mettle by spending a snowy winter's night in the hollow of a tree, an experience from which Harry emerges with his accustomed exuberance but which only stimulates in the over-refined Tommy the basest cravings for food, shelter, and warmth. In *Sandford and Merton,* Rousseau's idea of childhood and nature is tempered by numerous such eccentricities of detail and conception which make the book a good deal colder and more ominous than its French original. It is a very English book, nowhere more so than in the first meeting of Harry and Tommy: a snake winds itself around Tommy's leg while he is out walking, and Harry, more at ease with the natural world, intervenes and rescues his rich neighbor. In this case, of course, the snake represents ignorance of nature and not the knowledge of it offered by the serpent to Adam and Eve. But in the incident with the snake and a number of other details, Day's fable from Rousseau suggests the darker, more traditional view of nature and childhood which seems to inhere in English literature.

Whatever intimations and imitations of Rousseau's Pelagian vision of childhood there may have been in eighteenth-century English literature, it was Wordsworth who transformed the essentially French sentiments of *Emile* and the *Confessions,* from which Day and others had merely borrowed, into fundamentals of English poetics. But Wordsworth's approach to childhood, like his work as a whole, is far from monolithic and varies tellingly between his early and his late writing. He comes closest to Rousseau's idea of the child at the center of his career.

The early Wordsworth imitates Rousseau's picture of the child in many obvious respects ("In thoughtless gaiety I coursed the plain").[11] But even in early Wordsworth the accent on pathetic and solitary children often tempers the exuberance of *Emile* with a melancholy reminiscent of Gray and the orthodox handling of the child figure (in the later Wordsworth this tone will come to predominate):

> O blessed vision! happy child!
> Thou art so exquisitely wild,
> I think of thee with many fears
> For what may be thy lot in future years.
>
> .    .    .    .    .    .    .    .    .    .
>
> Thou art a dew-drop, which the morn brings forth
> Ill fitted to sustain unkindly shocks,
> Or to be trailed along the soiling earth.[12]

The contrast of fair infant and "soiling earth," while a commonplace in child elegies[13] before him, is not what the reader anticipates in the Wordsworth of "a sense sublime." Explicit here, the contrast lies dormant in most of his earliest work, and the first two books of *The Prelude* (1799) are more properly remembered as expressing his earliest vision of childhood:

> Oh, many a time have I, a five years' child,
> In a small mill-race severed from his stream,
> Made one long bathing of a summer's day;
> Basked in the sun, and plunged and basked again
> Alternate, all a summer's day, or scoured

The sandy fields, leaping through flowery groves
Of yellow ragwort; or when rock and hill,
The woods, and distant Skiddaw's lofty height,
Were bronzed with deepest radiance, stood alone‾
Beneath the sky, as if I had been born
On Indian plains, and from my mother's hut
Had run abroad in wantonness, to sport,
A naked savage, in the thunder shower.

(1.288–300)

For this child, who is a simultaneous realization of young
Emile at play and the noble savage,[14] the golden age is
continually present as a corporal entity, and that presence
is at once frightening and beautiful; it is also sanctified
by the Wisdom and Spirit of the universe, which

> didst intertwine for me
> The passions that build up our human soul;
> Not with the mean and vulgar works of man,
> But with high objects, with enduring things—
> With life and nature, purifying thus
> The elements of feeling and of thought,
> And sanctifying by such discipline,
> Both pain and fear, until we recognize
> A grandeur in the beatings of the heart.

(1.406–414)

The child of *The Prelude* is as mystical as the child of
Church dogma who is saved in baptism by prevenient
grace. Here, however, the mysticism lies in the child's
physical being, and the grace of which he is a model
resides not beyond the material world but at its core—in
the "grandeur in the beatings of the heart." Later in this
first book, Wordsworth speaks of the "organic pleasure"
experienced by the child, and throughout his early work,
it is an essential characteristic of the child that, whatever

the special nature of his intuition, it is gained by the purity and immediacy of his experiences in the physical world. His child is

> An inmate of this active universe:
> For feeling has to him imparted power
> That through the growing faculties of sense
> Doth like an agent of the one great Mind
> Create, creator and receiver both,
> Working but in alliance with the works
> Which it beholds.                    (2.254–260)

In early Wordsworth, childhood is full of the original innocence and sentiment which Rousseau had ascribed to it; but it is, unlike Rousseau's idea of childhood, not a state through which a man passes on his way toward a productive adulthood; it is a condition which for the vast majority of men is irretrievably lost as soon as completed:

> Such, verily, is the first
> Poetic spirit of our human life,
> By uniform control of after years,
> In most, abated or suppressed.
>                    (2.260–263)

This is not simply Rousseau's thesis that nature degenerates in the hands of social man. Wordsworth, in his early work, felt that the loss of the childhood state was a natural inevitability, as it had been in Marvell and Gray; childhood is a lost realm somewhere in the past of our lives and the past of our culture. Wordsworth makes the exception that in his poetic nature (and supposedly in others) the "infant sensibility" was "augmented and sustained" (2.270, 272). In this, the poet is separate from his fellow man and functions, like the *vates,* or poet-priest, of antiquity. Other men cannot experience or recall the essence of childhood; they may only know it vicariously as conjured by the poet, whose recollections

> almost make remotest infancy
> A visible scene, on which the sun is shining.
>
> (1.634–635)

The key word here is "almost." Though lived in flesh and blood, childhood for all but the poet, in whom it is "sustained," is as remote as Eden itself.

In the first four stanzas of Wordsworth's "Ode: Intimations of Immortality from Recollections of Early Childhood" (1807), this early vision of childhood has broken down: "The things which I have seen I now can see no more" (9). These first stanzas, written three or four years after the first books of *The Prelude,* speak of the loss of what had "sustained and augmented" his spirit earlier, the poet's privileged vision of childhood. Perhaps this loss is best understood not by the famous three lines which preface the poem ("The child is father of the Man . . ."), but by the six lines which preceded these in their original formulation of 1802, which are discarded for the purposes of the "Ode":

> My heart leaps up when I behold
> A rainbow in the sky:
> So was it when my life began;
> So is it now I am a man;
> So be it when I shall grow old,
> Or let me die!

These lines are dropped in the "Ode" because the poet's heart no longer leaps up and things are not as they were when his life began. By his earlier definition, this makes him no longer a poet, since to be a poet is to sustain the state of childhood. By the grand gesture of the early lines, he should now, at the time of the "Ode," be preparing himself for the death which ought to attend the loss of the childhood vision. The first stanzas of the "Ode" state this problem:

> Whither is fled the visionary gleam?
> Where is it now, the glory and the dream?
>
>                          (56–57)

The remainder of the "Ode," composed three to four years later than the first section, addresses itself to a solution of this riddle through a redefinition of the relationship between child and man.

This redefinition begins paradoxically in stanza 5 with a restatement of the idea of childhood as found in *The Prelude*: "Heaven lies about us in our infancy," the poet exclaims; the child is a noble savage whose intuitions of the physical world are sanctified by his rapport with the world spirit from whom he comes, "trailing clouds of glory." He is "Nature's Priest," just as the poet, when he "sustained" his childhood, was able to claim the role of poet-priest.

But nature and society soon begin camouflaging the inherent glory of the child:

> Earth fills her lap with pleasures of her own;
> Yearnings she hath in her own natural kind,
> And, even with something of a Mother's mind,
>          And no unworthy aim,
>          The homely Nurse doth all she can
> To make her Foster-child, her inmate Man,
> Forget the glories he had known,
> And that imperial palace whence he came.
>
>                          (Stanza 6)

The process of forgetting, however sad or cruel, is nonetheless a natural phenomenon which has now overtaken
the poet himself, and the middle section of the "Ode"
(stanzas 5 through 8) ends with a query as to why nature,
"with no unkindly aim," erases the memory of childhood
glory:

> Why with such earnest pains dost thou provoke
> The years to bring the inevitable yoke,
> Thus blindly with thy blessedness at strife?
>
> (127–129)

The final three stanzas reply to this question, and the
answer comes in a tone of triumph:

> O joy! that in our embers
> Is something that doth live,
> That nature yet remembers
> What was so fugitive!
>
> (133–136)

What is praised here is not childhood itself, but the remembrance of it:

> Delight and Liberty, the simple creed
> Of Childhood, whether busy or at rest,
> With new-fledged hope still fluttering in his breast:—
> Not for these I raise
> The song of thanks and praise.     (140–144)

Childhood itself with all its joys is incomplete and serves
no purpose unless it has a corresponding adulthood to
recall it, use it, and turn it to immediate advantage:

> Though inland far we be
> Our Souls have sight of that immortal sea
> Which brought us hither.
>
> (166–168)

In *The Prelude,* adulthood was regarded with dismay and suspicion; there, childhood was an end in itself. But here in the "Ode," the position has been reversed: childhood is not the goal, but a tool provided us (not just poets, but all of us) to accomplish the true, adult business of life:

> We will grieve not, rather find
> Strength in what remains behind;
> In the primal sympathy
> Which having been must ever be;
> In the soothing thoughts that spring
> Out of human suffering;
> In the faith that looks through death,
> In years that bring the philosophic mind.
>
> (183–190)

The poem, which begins like Tennyson's "Tithonus" in lamenting continued life without continued youth, ends like "Ulysses" in the assertion of the continuity, purpose, and joy implicit for the grown man in the "obstinate questionings" (145) which comprise the poem's early stanzas.

In the "Ode" Wordsworth is at his closest to Rousseau. Childhood is both good in itself and, properly tended, the seed from which useful, fulfilled man is necessarily grown. The sentiment the child evokes is not for our own lost youth, but for the immediate transcendence and joy available to us as adults through the vision of childhood. The child figure of Wordsworth in the "Ode," as in Rousseau, looks not backward to the lost Eden but forward to the "years that bring the philosophic mind."

Of course, as Wordsworth's idea of childhood shifts from *The Prelude*'s conception of a self-contained, mystic unit buried in the individual's past to the "Ode's" picture

of the symbiotic relationship between child and adult, he
is forced, like Rousseau, to attach increasingly greater
value to education. If childhood is, as the "Ode" pictures
it, the source upon which adulthood must draw those
recollections which illuminate the immediate moment,
then it is imperative that this source not be polluted. In
Books 8 and 9 of *The Excursion* (1814) Wordsworth deals
with this educational problem. In Book 8, the Wanderer
paints a grim picture of the children caught up in the
inhumanity of the industrial revolution:

> Can hope look forward to a manhood raised
> On such foundations?          (8.333–334)

To this, the Solitary replies that the industrial revolution
has not invented ignorance or degradation:

> Yet be it asked, in justice to our age,
> If there were not, before those arts appeared,
> These structures rose, commingling old and young,
> And unripe sex with sex, for mutual taint;
> If there were not, *then,* in our far-famed Isle,
> Multitudes, who from infancy had breathed
> Air unimprisoned, and had lived at large;
> Yet walked beneath the sun, in human shape,
> As abject as degraded?          (8.337–345)

The educational question raised by the "Ode" here forces
Wordsworth to consider the universal, and to the Solitary
at least, the pervasive sway of the "abject" and "degraded." In *The Excursion* this question is resolved in the
portraits of the pastor's son and the son's companion,
who, like Day's Harry Sandford, have the dual advantage
of nature and a parson to instruct them.

But the "Ode" had led Wordsworth to consider education in a darker and more serious vein than he had

before. In *The Prelude* "School-Time" (Book 2) had con-
sisted not so much in reading or lessons as in obtaining
"palpable access" (286) to nature, "seeking the visible
world" (278). But once the possibility had been acknowledged that childhood might be from the start "abject as
degraded," as Wordsworth is willing to admit in *The
Excursion,* education is no longer allowed the luxury of
being an extended exploration of nature in which the child
is trusted to reach the most felicitous conclusions. Instead,
education must be what Milton and orthodox Christianity
insisted it was, a means of repairing "the ruins of our
first parents."

After *The Excursion,* Wordsworth seems to have been
converted to an Augustinian position by these reflections.[15]
In *Ecclesiastical Sonnets* (1827), he takes the orthodox
position on baptism and the necessity for it due to man's
and nature's Fall:

> Dear be the Church that, watching o'er the needs
> Of Infancy, provides a timely shower
> Whose virtue changes to a Christian Flower
> A Growth from sinful Nature's bed of weeds!
>
> (Sonnet 20)

In the same year as this sonnet, he composed a sonnet
beginning, "Unquiet Childhood." In the end, Wordsworth
came around to the orthodox position on childhood; in
a sense, this is the failure of all late Wordsworth, that
these poems are the product of a poetic he himself had
sought to abolish. But at the same time, these late verses
of Wordsworth's demonstrate the resilience of the Augustinian child figure in English literature, a resilience which
is apparent throughout the nineteenth century and which
is all the more remarkable for its perseverance in the face

of the commanding Pelagian sentiment of the "Immortality Ode."

Blake, on having Wordsworth's "Ode" read to him, immediately perceived the nature of the heresy it contained: "I fear Wordsworth loves nature," he said, "and nature is the work of the Devil. The Devil is in us as far as we are nature."[16] The devil in man and nature haunts the pages of Blake's *Songs of Innocence* (1789), where he is disguised behind the very innocence Wordsworth glorifies. This devil is very much present in the bitter irony of "The Chimney Sweeper," where the young sweep, whose mother is dead and whose father has sold him into a virtual form of slavery, recounts Tom Dacre's vision of a happy, transcendent realm where redeemed sweeps lead the life of young Emile or the young Wordsworth of *The Prelude:*

> And by came an Angel who had a bright key,
> And he open'd the coffins & set them all free;
> Then down a green plain leaping, laughing, they run,
> And wash in a river, and shine in the Sun.
> Then naked & white, all their bags left behind,
> They rise upon clouds and sport in the wind;
> And the Angel told Tom, if he'd be a good boy,
> He'd have God for his father, & never want joy.

The Angel's vision is sufficient to reconcile the "innocent" sweep to the daily horrors of his trade, and even to turn him into a propagandist, inventing hopeful excuses to subdue the natural despair of his fellow sweeps:

> There's little Tom Dacre, who cried when his head
> That curl'd like a lamb's back, was shave'd: so I said
> "Hush, Tom! never mind it, for when your head's bare,
> You know that the soot cannot spoil your white hair."

Blake had complained that to be reconciled to nature was the devil's work; in the *Songs of Innocence,* the devil's triumph is to reconcile men to a mere vision of nature. The visionary innocence of the young sweep is all the more soul destroying for Blake because it affects our judgment with the kind of heretical sentiment pioneered by Rousseau and championed by Wordsworth. In "The Chimney-Sweep" Blake sees what Wordsworth did not till he had written his "Ode" and come to *The Excursion*— that innocence is at least partially ignorance, and ignorance merely perpetuates the existing enormities of the sweep's life and the world at large. In Blake's sense, nature is doubly fallen—not only is the natural environment of the sweep corrupt, but the joyous natural world he envisions is a misrepresentation of what is in truth a lapsed world. The final line of the poem ("So if all do their duty they need not fear harm") revolves on the interpretation of "duty"—duty to whom, God or the Devil? Blake felt that the duty done by the innocent sweep was the worship of Wordsworth's devil.

If the chimney sweeper of the *Songs of Innocence* paints a joyous picture of despair, there is at least a desperate hope attached to his companion in the *Songs of Experience* (1794):

> A little black thing among the snow,
> Crying "'weep! 'weep!" in notes of woe!
> "Where are thy father & mother? say?"
> "They are both gone up to the church to pray.
>
> "Because I was happy upon the heath
> And smil'd among the winter's snow,
> They clothed me in the clothes of death,
> And taught me to sing the notes of woe.

"And because I am happy & dance & sing,
They think they have done me no injury,
And are gone to praise God & his Priest & King,
Who make up a heaven of our misery."

The poem of experience is, by a Blakean paradox, much simpler than that of innocence. The hope and strength of the poem come from the sweep's perception of the fallen condition, a perception which allows him, when left alone, to smile in the winter snow. The hypocrisies of the angel's vision are gone. Nature is a harsh reality, but understood as such, it is possible to be happy within it. Here at least the sweep is imprisoned by corrupt earthly agents, not by his own false impressions. His clearer understanding of the situation is a kind of grace, a true baptism by which to lift himself from the fallen state.

Behind much of Blake's genius, considered by many of his contemporaries to be "insane" (the term is Wordsworth's),[17] lie the orthodox teachings of the Church. The Augustinian belief in the originally sinful nature of man and the world he has corrupted is one of these beliefs,[18] demonstrated in Blake's use of the child figure as well as in his prophetic writings:

wherever a grass grows
Or a leaf buds, The Eternal Man is seen, is heard, is felt,
And all his sorrows, till he reassumes his ancient bliss.
(*The Four Zoas*, "Night the Ninth," 582–584)

From Blake's orthodox beliefs—in Original Sin, in the desperate nature of man's sojourn on earth, in the nearness of the Second Coming by which we regain our "ancient bliss"—a special kind of sentiment evolves in which our sympathies are set in motion not so much by the innocence of children as by the inevitability of their corruption, the agents of which are marshalled about them in seemingly impenetrable array. Our hopes for salvation in this situation must necessarily take on an apocalyptic character, which is quite manifest in Blake's major works.

Blake is in the main tradition of English letters in using the child to connote both the lost Eden and the coming Apocalypse. He is unique in his use of Wordsworth's kind of sentiment to debunk Wordsworth's view of nature and innocence; the introductory poem of *Songs of Innocence* gives a child figure similar in feeling and content to the child of the "Immortality Ode," who comes "trailing clouds of glory." Blake says,

> On a cloud I saw a child
> And he laughing said to me:
> "Pipe a song about a Lamb!"
> So I piped with merry cheer.

Later, in *Songs of Experience,* the sentiment of merry cheer will be undercut when the child himself speaks:

> My mother groan'd! my father wept.
> Into the dangerous world I leapt:
> Helpless, naked, piping loud:
> Like a fiend hid in a cloud.
>                    ("Infant Sorrow")

Whatever cheer is possible for man does not lie in the simple, immediate joys of the laughing child, behind whom a fiend is hidden. The Wordsworthian child of the present moment is, like the child of one poem's title, "The Little Girl Lost"; the "merry cheer" of the *Songs* comes in the prophetic future:

In futurity
I prophetic see
That the earth from sleep
(Grave the sentence deep)
Shall arise and seek
For her maker meek;
And the desert wild
Become a garden mild.

By the first decade of the nineteenth century, the child figure was established as a vehicle through which the traditional questions which in Christian doctrine cluster around the concept of Original Sin—man's innocence or lack of it, his relation to nature, and his need for salvation—might be discussed. As the century opened, the child figure offered both a realistic literary image by which these questions could be pursued and a forum for continuing the Pelagian controversy which had consumed the attention of the Church 1,500 years before. For the Fathers of the Church, however, the child had been an object of philosophic and dogmatic dispute; for the nineteenth century, the child was an object of sentiment. Wordsworth and Blake, approaching the child from classically opposed directions, both employ the child figure not to make their readers understand a truth, but to make them feel it.

Because the child figure became a tool for conflicting schools of sentiment, we cannot follow the progress of this conflict through neat philosophical pronouncements such as the Council of Carthage provided in the fifth century dispute. Instead, it is necessary to see how people reacted to the child figure and to which type of sentiment—Wordsworth's or Blake's—audiences were more responsive.

A convenient index of the response to the child figure is the social legislation enacted in nineteenth-century England as a result of increased interest in and concern with childhood. What was the emotional impetus behind this drive to reform the social image of childhood? In 1676, 51 percent of infant mortality in London was attributed to starvation; in 1767 Jonas Hanway computed that of the 2,415 children left to the exclusive care of the parishes of London in a three-year period (1762–65), only 690 survived the experience.[19] Not until the nineteenth century did statistics like these—and the scenes of daily life which must have accompanied them—evoke enough concern to be transformed into prohibitive legislation. But what was the nature of that concern?

Anthony Ashley Cooper, the seventh Lord Shaftesbury, was the leading political champion and public spokesman for legislation aimed at eliminating the abuses to which children were subjected in the nineteenth century. A proper Tory and evangelical Anglican, his model of a statesman was Wellington; of a poet, Southey. He opposed the Reform Bill, the admission of Jews into Parliament, the franchise for women, and the English Revised Version of the Bible, commissioned as it was by a Liberal government. An appallingly stuffy man, he bored even the Queen. Yet when he died in 1885, the Duke of Argyll said of him that "the social reforms of the last century have not been mainly due to the Liberal party. They have been due mainly to the influence, character, and perseverance of one man—Lord Shaftesbury."[20] Though the Duke spoke with a Tory bias, he seems very nearly to have spoken the truth. Shaftesbury was the moving force behind the passage of the Factory Acts, the ragged schools, abolition, the suppression of the opium trade, the establishment of Sunday schools. He refused a position in a succession of Tory governments, and his forum for urging reform was, first, the public platform and only secondly the back benches. He was equally to be found at charitable balls, prayer meetings, union halls, and tract societies. In 1848, at their request, he met with four hundred London thieves to hear their complaints and aspirations. At his funeral, held in Westminster Abbey, his biographer records that strong men wept, that the band from the Costermonger's Temperance Society solemnly performed "Safe in the Arms of Jesus," that the rabble freely mixed with nobles and gentlemen in a communion of grief, and that one laborer, overcome by the sorrow of the whole proceeding, cried out, "Our Earl's gone! God A'mighty knows he loved us, and we loved him." [21] The sentiments Shaftesbury espoused were certainly not the only ones possible in Victorian England, but they were the ones which summoned up enough emotional response to pass legislation—so much so that in terms of political accomplishment, the seventh Lord Shaftesbury's pious zeal makes the first Lord Shaftesbury's Machiavellian acumen seem like a thing of little effect.

What were the Victorian Lord Shaftesbury's sentiments? "There is very little seeming, and no real, hope for mankind but in the Second Advent; all our efforts are weak and transitory, and issue in works very little stronger or more lasting—if we succeed in any project having for its end the good of the human race." [22] The Second Coming is a recurring theme in Shaftesbury's diaries, his one source of consolation, and the foundation of his religious and political drive: "Oh that it were so in the providence of God that the intervening 'days should be shortened' and a speedy and closer limit be set to the sins, and coming sufferings, of mankind!''[23] The man who more than any other epitomized philanthropy, charity, and the humane spirit in Victorian England viewed his work as a losing battle against irresistible, evil forces. Behind his efforts lay a mystical, apocalyptic view of society and religion, a marriage of Tory gloom and evangelical piety.

"Evil is more powerful and lasting than good; evil is natural, good is unnatural; evil requires nothing but man as he is, good must find the soil prepared by the grace of God," he wrote in his diary while vacationing, in upper-class Victorian fashion, by the sea at Brighton.[24] Augustinian to the core, he looked about at the misery and vice of nineteenth-century England, saw that it was hopeless, and changed it anyway. This was the politics of sentiment. Behind the effusions of his funeral, behind the countless outpourings of emotion and feeling of which he was the object during a lifetime of public service—which are often grotesquely overblown—there is a sense of doom, a taste of wormwood. Small wonder Shaftesbury's brand of sentiment brought a tear to the eye.

In his political career and philanthropic endeavors, Shaftesbury's sentimentalism attached itself to the plight of the child with remarkable frequency. Considering the nature of his sentimentalism, this is hardly surprising. As we have seen, social philosophy based on the Augustinian concerns of Original Sin, universal corruption, and the mystical possibilities of divine grace easily elevates the child to a place of special importance, just as the issue of infant baptism easily becomes a focal point for these doctrines in the dogma of the Church. In a sense, Shaftesbury's entire political program aims at a general baptism of society, a remission of sins, and regeneration through divine grace parliamentarily administered. The Factory Act of 1847 is a remarkable example. This central piece of nineteenth-century legislation, which is regarded as the first step in the weary attempt to humanize and control the industrial revolution, was not an act which helped or provided for the working man in any way. As much as the radicals and socialists identified their interests with those of the act, they profited only vicariously by its passage. The Factory Act of 1847, for which Ashley was so largely responsible, provided only for children, setting limits to the working hours of thirteen-year-olds and under and providing for their education.

But perhaps Shaftesbury's pet cause was the regulation of the chimney-sweepers. The sweeps, whose trade was essential in a society dependent on the hearth for food and warmth, were generally under twelve, illiterate, unwashed, housed in soot piles, and fed at their masters' whim. They were subject to the vicious "chimney sweeper's cancer" which afflicted the scrotum with boils and required castration to halt its progress. Though the sweeps had been a feature of English life from the introduction of the flue in the Tudor period, these abuses called forth a response only gradually: Hanway writes of them in 1785; James Montgomery compiled an anthology of prose and verse addressed to the horrors of the trade (1824);[25] and of course Blake had used the chimney sweep in his *Songs*. It remained for Shaftesbury to translate the sentiment of Blake's poems into political action. In 1840 he lobbied for the Chimney Sweepers' Regulation Act, which was generally believed to have done away with the fouler inhumanities of the trade. It failed; in 1861 Henry Mayhew could describe the sweeps' condition in terms exactly like those Hanway had used seventy-five years earlier.[26] In 1875, after years of attempts, Shaftesbury finally introduced and passed an act to eliminate once and for all the abuses of the trade.

None of Shaftesbury's reforms for children would have been possible without the massive public support he was capable of stimulating, and this support in turn could never have been forthcoming unless Shaftesbury and his public enjoyed a common bond of sentiment and sympathy. In Shaftesbury, these sentiments were decidedly Augustinian, and, though Shaftesbury might be amazed, very much in accord with Blake's. It is natural to suppose that Shaftesbury's public responded to his reforms out of shared sentiments. As noted before, the Augustinian notion of Original Sin and the child figure derived from it seem to have favored status in English literature; it is not surprising this status should extend to English life as well. The following chapters will look at a number of Victorian child figures, almost all of which will be indebted to the Augustinian image of childhood and the tradition of sentiment in which Shaftesbury is the political champion. The joyous, transcendent immediacy of Rousseau's and the early Wordsworth's children has attracted many admirers and few imitators. As regards the vision of childhood and the kind of sentiment which in English literature envelops the child, Wordsworth seems destined to play the role of a Pelagius, championing the ideas of an older belief even while they are in the process of yielding to new ones:

Great God! I'd rather be
A Pagan suckled in a creed outworn;
So might I, standing on this pleasant lea,
Have glimpses that would make me less forlorn.

# IV

# The Children of Dickens,
# George Eliot, and Henry James

The fate of Dickens's Little Nell was a matter of such
grave public concern that throngs lined the pier in New
York awaiting the final installment of *The Old Curiosity
Shop* (1840–1841) to learn if she had lived or died, while
in England her demise unleased a sentimental furor.
Carlyle was overcome, Daniel O'Connell and Lord Jeffrey
wept bitterly.[1] Tears were the order of the day. But what
inspired melancholy in the last century now serves to evoke
contempt; so *The Old Curiosity Shop* becomes for a modern critic "cruelly dated," "Dickens' least successful novel,
a work in which he seems to have lost much of his intellectual control, abandoning himself to all that was
weakest and least mature in his character as a writer."[2]

Yet the sentiment that characterizes *The Old Curiosity
Shop* can be found everywhere in Dickens, even in his
strongest and most mature works, and often in doses more
mawkish. One example—Bella's announcement to John of
her pregnancy in *Our Mutual Friend* (1864–65)—should
be sufficient to establish the point:

> As he bent his face to hers, she raised hers to meet
> it, and laid her little right hand on his eyes, and kept
> it there.
> "Do you remember, John, on the day we were
> married, Pa's speaking of the ships that might be sailing
> towards us from the unknown seas?"

76

"Perfectly, my darling!"

"I think . . . among them . . . there is a ship upon the ocean . . . bringing . . . to you and me . . . a little baby, John." (4.5)

The worst that can be said about *The Old Curiosity Shop* is that its sentiment is more sustained and more affecting than elsewhere in Dickens.

What is missing in *The Old Curiosity Shop* is not the strength and genius which characterizes Dickens's other work, but the intricacy and intensity of plot which mark his better-known novels. The framework of the story, which in all his later novels provides mystery, excitement, and motive force, is here vague and unimportant. The Single Gentleman's explanation of Nell's ancestry, the sort of explanation which in the earlier *Oliver Twist* is at once necessary to the book's premise and conclusion, is in *The Old Curiosity Shop* pointless. It explains very little of what actually occurs in the novel and does nothing at all toward resolving the action. The flight of the child and her grandfather from London is made on the slenderest grounds. Quilp's evil plots hinge on the very tentative delusion that Nell, considered by some (themselves minor figures in the society of London) to be an heiress, is in fact going to turn out to be a pauper. What is lacking here is the grandeur Dickens brings to later plots—say in the fall of Lady Dedlock, which is not only spectacular in itself but involves every corner of society and every aspect of the novel. This lack of cohesive plotting in *The Old Curiosity Shop* draws attention to its unrelieved vistas of sentiment, whereas in his other writing the sentiment clings to the plot structure like flesh to the bone.

It would be fruitless to attempt making the lack of plot

in the novel seem like an ingenious stroke of artistry.
It obviously weakens the book and leaves it open to the
criticisms which have been lavished on it. But at least
there is good reason to believe that Dickens achieved in
*The Old Curiosity Shop* exactly what he set out to do:
the book is a continuation of *Master Humphrey's Clock,*
which Dickens intended to be nothing more organized
than a series of "detached papers." [3] Poor sales prompted
him to produce a continuous narrative, however. But
his intention had originally been to leave plot aside for
a while and work on the development of theme, style,
and substance, which is exactly what he does in *The Old
Curiosity Shop.* Nor is the reference to *Pilgrim's Progress*
in chapter 15 accidental; the analogy is meant to be drawn.
By making his novel picaresque, by substituting pilgrimage
for plot, Dickens freed himself to experiment with the uses
not simply of sentiment but of Bunyanesque imagery.
Viewed as such an experiment, the novel gains a certain
interest, if not success.

Central to this experiment is the figure of the child,
Little Nell. In *The Old Curiosity Shop* Dickens is quite
consciously using the child as an evocative literary device;
he wrote Forster during the composition of the book,
"As to the child-image, I have made a note of it for
alteration." [4] Throughout the story, he speaks not of Nell
and her grandfather, but of "the child" and "the old
man." At this point in his career, Dickens was studying
the basic structure which underlies the outward trappings
of characterization, the ideas and sentiments which adhere
to certain character types, and the uses to which they
could be put.

Clearly, the source and manipulation of the sentiment

which surrounds the child figure was very much on
Dickens's mind in creating Little Nell. He had before him
the sentimental examples of Wordsworth as well as the
Augustinian tradition of child depiction represented by
Gray, Blake, and Shakespeare. The finished characterization of Little Nell suggests that he used both strains of
sentiment, fashioning them into a highly emotional literary
vehicle by which his audience could be made not simply
to understand his views on man's role in a fallen world,
but to feel them as well.

Dickens is often capable of touches purely Wordsworthian in *The Old Curiosity Shop,* as in the following
passage, which might be a paraphrase of the sonnet,
"Composed Upon Westminster Bridge": "It was the
beginning of a day in June; the deep blue sky unsullied
by a cloud, and teeming with brilliant light. The streets
were, as yet, nearly free from passengers, the houses and
shops were closed, and the healthy air of morning fell
like breath from angels, on the sleeping town" (12).
Except for the angels' breath, this is Wordsworth's
London, beautiful only when "silent, bare," and thus open
to the benign influences of nature's air and light. Yet
more often, Dickens's effusions on nature add a touch of
gloom which alters the Wordsworthian tone: "Oh! the
glory of the sudden burst of light; the freshness of the
fields and woods, stretching away on every side, and
meeting the bright blue sky; the cattle grazing in the
pasturage; the smoke, that, coming from among the trees,
seemed to rise upward from the green earth; the children
yet at their gambols down below—all, everything, so
beautiful and happy! It was like passing from death to
life; it was drawing nearer to Heaven" (53). Nell's joyous

revery on her natural surroundings is tempered by the fact that she observes all this from the tower of a gloomy Gothic church surrounded by the tombstones, among which she finds such happiness in frolicking, and that in the larger scheme of the book, passing from death to life and drawing nearer to Heaven will involve her own death. This contradiction, in which nature appears as a humble substitute for some more sublime, heavenly reality, obtainable only through dying, appears again and again in Dickens. It is an idea which gives a very un-Wordsworthian turn to the language of Wordsworth.

The figure of the child is an extension of these sentiments on nature. Her innocence, like the innocence and beauty of nature, is somehow fatal, and critics who have found the character of Little Nell deadly come closer to the mark than they know. Possessed of every virtue, pure beyond the sympathies of modern audiences, she can no more pass a graveyard than an alcoholic can a bar. Forster takes credit for the idea of finishing her off at the end of the book, in order "to lift her also out of the commonplace of ordinary happy endings, so that the gentle, pure little figure and form should never change to the fancy," [5] and Dickens readily accepted his suggestion. Innocent children always have a certain morbid quality in Dickens, even those that he permits to survive (the mortality rate is quite steep among Dickens's children).

The significance of these deadly innocents is enmeshed in the larger structure of Dickens's imagery, and in *The Old Curiosity Shop* as elsewhere in his work, is intimately related to the figures of the old man and the city. Dickens has a certain type of old man, of which Nell's grandfather is one, which is best described by a piece of Chaucer criticism: Robert Miller's identification of the old man of "The Pardoner's Tale" with the *vetus homo* of St. Paul is useful well beyond the medieval period.[6] Nor would Dickens have to prove a Chaucerian scholar or a devotee of exigetical theology to be aware of the possibilities of this image. His devotion to the New Testament and Bunyan were sufficient to establish major Christian images in his work; he was the master of the "broad spirit" of Christianity.[7]

The concept of the old man, fully elaborated by Miller, rests on a connection of several passages of the epistles, most importantly Romans: "Our old man is crucified with him, that the body of sin might be destroyed, that henceforth we should not serve sin" (6:6). The discussion of the *vetus homo* is introduced in the Pauline explanation of the connection between sin and the Old Law of the Jews, a system replaced by Christ's redemption of man from the rule of this law, and with it, from sin itself. Traditionally, these passages are linked with the idea of the Old and the New Adam presented in 1 Corinthians 15: "The first man Adam was made a living soul; the last Adam was made a quickening spirit. . . . The first man is of the earth, earthy: the second man is the Lord from heaven" (45, 47). There is no need to establish Dickens's familiarity with these texts. His knowledge of the New Testament is remarkably demonstrated everywhere in his writing. His use of old men is convincing enough in itself to show that, consciously or not, he had made the connection between these various passages, the same passages on which so much of St. Augustine's theology likewise depends.

The old man figure occurs with regularity in Dickens,

the most outstanding examples being Nell's grandfather, Scrooge, Fagin, and Riah. With the last two, the connection with the Old Law is emphasized by the fact that they are Jews, living under the Old Dispensation. In *The Old Curiosity Shop,* the theme of the Old Adam, trapped under a law which is the rule of sin, is especially emphasized by the repetition of the operative word *old.* Not only is the grandfather referred to as an old man, but he is the proprietor of the "old curiosity shop" which gives the book its title, "one of those receptacles for old and curious things which seem to crouch in odd corners of this town, and to hide their musty treasures from the public eye in jealousy and distrust" (1). The embodiment of the old man's enslavement to the Old Law is his addiction to gambling, referred to in the page headings of chapter twenty-nine as "The Old Temptation" and "The Old Distorted Faith," and indeed it is this weakness which subjects him to the malign influences of the law itself, as represented by the Brass family. Here as elsewhere in Dickens the law which is practiced by attorneys such as Brass is indeed the Old Law, replete with "the motions of sins" (Rom. 7:5), which "bring forth fruit unto death."

The figure of the *vetus homo* never appears in Dickens without its counterpart, the child. Fagin has his Oliver, the owner of the curiosity shop his Nell, Scrooge his Tiny Tim, and Riah his Jenny Wren. In each case, the old man is redeemed from outright condemnation by the interest he has for the child figure; each of these *veteres homines* is virtually a Tithonus, consumed by a cruel immortality thrust upon them from without. Unlike Tithonus, however, these old men have at hand a means of release from their "old distorted faith" in the figure of the child.

By the obvious parallel, the child then becomes a type of the regenerate man, the New Dispensation, the New Adam. With this parallel in mind, the morbidness of so many of Dickens's children is more easily explicable: these children are ultimately the precursors of new life, but a kind of new life which in Dickens's version of Christian imagery is a product of death. In fact, the morbidity of *The Old Curiosity Shop* stems not so much from its dwelling upon death, but from its rhapsodic assessment of what death is. The graveyard in which Little Nell loves to pass the idle hour is "another world, where sin and sorrow never came; a tranquil place of rest, where nothing evil entered" (54), and the end of life is eulogized in these terms: "Forgotten! oh, if the good deeds of human creatures could be traced to their source, how beautiful would even death appear; for how much charity, mercy, and purified affection would be seen to have their growth in dusty graves!" (54). The idea, spoken through the kindly old schoolmaster, is more truly Dickens's own. Such emotions, standing side by side with a seemingly Wordsworthian glorification of life, give the novel the strength of a profound contradiction, one from which the sentimental potency of Little Nell derives: her death is at once a tragedy and an essential element in the larger and triumphant pattern of the divine comedy. Today the reader may be offended or amused by the purple prose of the following passage, yet there is no ignoring the sincerity with which it was written or the central place it holds in bringing together the themes and imagery of the novel:

> Oh! it is hard to take to heart the lesson that such deaths [Little Nell's in this instance] will teach, but let no man reject it, for it is one that all must learn, and is a mighty, universal Truth. When Death strikes down

the innocent and young, for every frail form from which he lets the panting spirit free, a hundred virtues rise, in shapes of mercy, charity, and love, to walk the world, and bless it. Of every tear that sorrowing mortals shed on such green graves, some good is born, some gentler nature comes. In the Destroyer's steps there spring up bright creations that defy his power, and his dark path becomes a way of light to Heaven.        (72)

In his later work, when these themes of death and regeneration became embedded in the environment of the Victorian city, it was a natural step to reinforce the imagery with another concept that might equally have come from the pages of Augustine, the idea of a heavenly and an earthly city. Jenny Wren, Nell's counterpart in *Our Mutual Friend,* is unlike her predecessor entrenched in the dark industrial world of mid-nineteenth-century England (her sadistic imagination is undoubtedly a product of this environment). Since she never leaves London, all the thematic work which surrounds the child figure of Little Nell is in her incorporated into the image of the city. Like Nell, Jenny is a peculiarly morbid creature, but her taste for death has found a milieu more realistic and forceful than the graveyard scenes in which Nell exercises her melancholy innocence. In *Our Mutual Friend,* the city has become the graveyard, and though there is a preoccupation with death equal to that of *The Old Curiosity Shop,* it is redeemed from the charge of sloppy sentiment by being firmly rooted in the images not only of the child and the old man, but of the city itself:

"How do you feel when you are dead?" asked Fledgeby, much perplexed.
"Oh, so tranquil!" cried the little creature, smiling.

"Oh, so peaceful and so thankful! And you hear the
people who are live, crying, and working, and calling
to one another down in the close dark streets, and
you seem to pity them so! And such a chain has fallen
from you, and such a strange good sorrowful happiness
comes upon you!"

Her eyes fell on the old man, who, with his hands
folded, quietly looked on.      (2.5)

The chapter ends with the most hopeful and lovely sentiment the "little creature" knows how to lavish on the
kindly old Riah, as she invites him to return to the roof
where they look over the grey, earthly city: "Come up
and be dead!" she cries. "Come up and be dead!"

These figures of the child and old man are not the
figures of allegory. Again and again they will defy simple
equation with any set of values or any attempt to predict
their use and behavior. Tiny Tim lives while Paul Dombey
dies. Jenny Wren lives on where Little Nell passes over.
Scrooge is a Christian; Fagan, a Jew. The essential element
in each case is not the uniform character or behavior of
the figure, but the uniformity with which it evokes a set
of ideas. Paul Dombey summons up much the same series
of questions and answers as Oliver Twist concerning the
possibilities of goodness in a substantially corrupted
world, yet they are as unlike in character as is the
handling of this central theme in the two works in which
they appear. Consistency in the pattern of literary figures
is not to be found in the allegorical equation of characters
with concepts, but rather in the overall scheme of ideas
embodied in the figures and worked out to similar
conclusions.

With the figures of the child and old man, it is impossible to generalize and say that the child always dies, though this is often the case. It is possible, however, when viewing the child as an integral part of a complex inter-action of images and ideas, to see that the child figure only survives where the forces of the Old Dispensation, so frequently represented by old men, are either regener-ated or destroyed. Tiny Tim's crutch would be hanging by the hearth today if Scrooge were still the cruel miser he had been. Where there is no reform of the Old Law, Little Nell is condemned to die, the promise of salvation she represents going unused by man. This use of the child to represent the need and potential for redemption is equally apparent in the figure of Jo in *Bleak House* (1852–53), who is privileged to have a glimpse of Augus-tine's heavenly city superimposed over the very earthly industrial London:

> And there he sits, munching and gnawing, and look-ing up at the great Cross on the summit of St. Paul's Cathedral, glittering above a red and violet-tinted cloud of smoke. From the boy's face one might suppose that sacred emblem to be, in his eyes, the crowning con-fusion of the great, confused city; so golden, so high up, so far out of his reach. There he sits, the sun going down, the river running fast, the crowd flowing by him in two streams—everything moving on to some purpose and to one end—until he is stirred up, and told to "move on" too.                                            (19)

Like Little Nell, Jo has a footing in the "out of reach" heavenly city, and when the earthly cruelties that the novel portrays prevent the realization of the heavenly realm in the material world, Jo is indeed obliged to "move on" in order to reach the "one end" toward which everything is directed. "Moving on" for Jo means what it had for

Little Nell—death. Jo's death is a tragedy not so much
for Jo, who moves into the realm of light, but for his
survivors, who forfeit in the death of the child figure one
means of salvation:

> The light is come upon the dark benighted way.
> Dead!
> Dead, your Majesty. Dead, my lords and gentlemen.
> Dead, Right Reverends and Wrong Reverends of every
> order. Dead, men and women, born with Heavenly
> compassion in your hearts. And dying thus around us
> every day. (47)

The gush of sentiment in this and other passages of
Dickens shouldn't blind us to the fact that Dickens
means exactly what he says in these outpourings: there is
a heavenly city of light which is obtainable in this world
by freeing ourselves from the bondage of the Old Law;
but failing this, the only avenue to the heavenly city lies
through the destruction of the physical body itself.

In *Dombey and Son* (1846–1848), which has rightly been
called the turning point in Dickens's career, his concern
with the Old and New Law, regeneration, the return to
Eden, and the heavenly city are treated in an epic framework, over which the child presides in a manner akin to
the way in which Gloriana presides over *The Faerie
Queene*. In *The Old Curiosity Shop* Dickens dealt with the
theme of fallen man in terms of character and literary
image without a substantial plot to bind them into a whole,
but in *Dombey* character and image operate within a structure loosely modeled on *Paradise Lost*.

The presence of Milton is so strongly felt in *Dombey
and Son* that it is tantamount to an announcement that
Dickens is working in the epic style. In chapter 47, he

goes so far as to render the invocation to Book Four of
*Paradise Lost* into high Victoriana: "Oh, for a good
spirit who would take the house-tops off, with a more
potent and benignant hand than the lame demon in the
tale, and show a Christian people what dark shapes issue
from amidst their homes to swell the retinue of the
Destroying Angel as he moves forth among them!" Edith
and her mother, whom "Nature intended for an Arcadian,"
are constantly discussing Eden, "the garden of what's-its-
name," and having found in Edith a latter-day Eve,
Dickens copies her deceiver, Carker, almost line for line
from the great Miltonic original. Carker, inhibited by the
boundaries of realism, cannot turn into a tiger, lion, cor-
morant, or serpent at will, but he is constantly referred
to as a cat; "a cat, or a monkey, or a hyena, or a
death's head" (17); and in the scene which parallels Satan's
first sighting of Adam and Eve, his meditations "kept
close to their nest upon the earth, and [he] looked about,
among the dust and worms" (27). He cannot bodily be
placed in the Tree of Life, but he may stroll "about
meadows, and green lanes," and glide "among avenues of
trees" directly before he chooses to meet the new Mrs.
Dombey, his Eve.

Satan's address to the sun is also easily incorporated:

> He turned to where the sun was rising, and behind it,
> in its glory, as it broke upon the scene.
>
> So awful, so transcendent in its beauty, so divinely
> solemn. As he cast his faded eyes upon it, where it
> rose, tranquil and serene, unmoved by all the wrong
> and wickedness on which its beams had shone since
> the beginning of the world, who shall say that some
> weak sense of virtue upon earth, and its reward in
> Heaven, did not manifest itself, even to him?    (55)

Nor has Dickens missed Milton's connection of the Fall and the Apocalypse in Book Four:

> O for that warning voice, which he who saw
> Th' Apocalypse, heard cry in Heav'n aloud,
> Then when the Dragon, put to second route,
> Came furious down to be reveng'd on men.

In *Dombey and Son* the dragon of Revelation and the Satan of Genesis coexist: the "tame dragons" (15) of the novel being the railroad trains, which make the walls quake, "as if they were dilating with the secret knowledge of great powers yet unsuspected in them, and strong purposes not yet achieved." While Carker goes about his business of original corruption, the railway, as if the seven vials had just been poured, is paving the way for the new heaven and the new earth: "Houses were knocked down; streets broken through and stopped; deep pits and trenches dug in the ground; enormous heaps of earth and clay thrown up. . . . Hot springs and fiery eruptions, the usual attendants upon earthquakes, lent their contributions of confusion to the scene. Boiling water hissed and heaved within dilapidated walls, whence, also, the glare and roar of flames came issuing forth" (6). So mighty an earthquake, and so great! Dickens's new Jerusalem should be ushered in by the Exterminating Angel, and Dickens does not hesitate to call his railroad Death. The Miltonic parallel is complete when,

> like a devilish engine back recoils
> Upon itself,

Carker is destroyed under the wheels of the train.

Within the Miltonic framework of *Dombey and Son,* it is the son of the title who plays the role of Christ in

*Paradise Lost.* Little Paul Dombey, though his part is often played offstage or from beyond the grave, like Christ's role in Milton's epic or in Christian theology, is the pivotal figure of the novel. Dickens purposely associates him with Christ, and as Paul dies, he is pictured as looking upon Jesus in heaven: "Tell them that the print upon the stairs at the school is not divine enough" (16), he says, expiring. In Paul's death, as in Christ's, time is gathered up and united in a single, eternal moment of grace; from his curiously passive presence and pathetic death, the novel's grand design of salvation for fallen man proceeds. His death sets in motion the events and alterations in character which lead to Carker's demise, Dombey's regeneration, and, by implication, the prospect of that immortality which had been Christ's gift of grace. At Paul's death, Dickens is explicit on this point, referring both to the Fall and the promise of redemption while the reader has the picture of Paul's death fresh in his mind:

> The old, old fashion! The fashion that came in with our first garments, and will last unchanged until our race has run its course, and the wide firmament is rolled up like a scroll. The old, old fashion—Death!
>
> O thank GOD, all who see it, for that older fashion yet, of Immortality! And look upon us, angels of young children, with regards not quite estranged, when the swift river bears us to the ocean!                    (16)

To complete the pattern of Christian imagery, young Paul comes again on the latter day in the person of Florence's son, also named Paul. This Second Coming coincides with the elder Dombey's redemption and the book's ending; by this point, the novel has presumably demonstrated the total movement from the acquisition of man's "first garments" in Eden to the rolling up of the heavens "like a scroll." Here, as elsewhere, the child figure is not only important in himself, but as a symptom of the kinds of imagery and themes which will develop around him.

The question of the part played by Paul's father in this cosmic drama remains. If Carker is a Satan, Edith a fallen Eve, and Paul a Christ, what is Dombey himself? As Edith's husband he is necessarily cast in the role of the fallen Adam, and indeed, his pride is so monstrous that, like Adam's sin, it encompasses all others. He is the Old Adam of St. Paul who is saved by the intervention and mediation of Christ, here played by his son. But he is also Paul's father, and by virtue of this he should, in the parallelism of the novel, also be God himself. This is a role the elder Dombey has no trouble pretending to play (in chapter I Dickens says of him, "Common abbreviations took new meaning in his eyes, and had sole reference to them: A.D. had no concern with anno Domini, but stood for anno Dombei—and Son").

The father of *Dombey and Son* is not only the Old Adam, but the Old Adam's patriarchal God, the proud father who presides over the Old Covenant. In effect, the novel tells how the Ancient of Days becomes a kindly old grandfather to Christianity. Dickens had no love for the Old Testament God or his religion, which are represented in the novel by the deadly atmosphere of the church in which Dombey takes his son to be christened:

> Little Paul might have asked with Hamlet "into my grave?"—so chill and earthly was the place. The tall shrouded pulpit and reading desk; the dreary perspective of empty pews stretching away under the galleries, and empty benches mounting to the roof and lost in the

shadow of the great grim organ; the dusty matting and
cold stone slabs; the grisly free seats in the aisles; and
the damp corner by the bell-rope, where the black tres-
sels used for funerals were stowed away, along with
some shovels and baskets, and a coil or two of deadly-
looking rope; the strange, unusual, uncomfortable
smell, and the cadaverous light were all in unison.

Nor is the sepulchral effect of the church a mere digression; in the chill, Paul contracts a cold which is the
beginning of his sickness and leads to his death. Dombey,
who is associated with the church throughout the chapter
through the cold—his rooms are cold, his manner is cold,
even the food at the reception he gives is cold—is ad-
monished by Dickens for his lack of Christian understanding during the baptism: "It might have been well for
Mr. Dombey if he had thought of his own dignity a little
less; and had thought of the great origin and purpose of
the ceremony, in which he took so formal and so stiff a
part, a little more. His arrogance contrasted strangely with
its history." Here Dickens and Milton part ways. The
stern Father of *Paradise Lost* was unacceptable to
Dickens, and in *Dombey and Son* he transforms that proud
figure, who after all administered the Old Law which
Christ had replaced, into the more pleasant, more affable
"white-haired gentleman" who "likes best to see the child
free and stirring" (62). The Dombey of the book's last
chapter might have stepped out of the pages of a Sunday
school primer. He is the God of Calvin and Carlyle as
processed through the novel's epic machinery and recon-
stituted as the God of Dickens. He is, of course, a God
who suffers the little children. But more especially, he
is the servant of young Paul, the child god.

Dickens's child figures are, of course, marked by flourishes uniquely his own. No other author has surpassed them in their ability to elicit a sentimental response, and many authors as well as readers have felt that Dickens's children mined a vein of pathos unworthy of good literature. Writing of Jenny Wren, Henry James remarked that "like all Mr. Dickens's pathetic characters, she is a little monster; she is deformed, unhealthy, unnatural; she belongs to the troop of hunchbacks, imbeciles, and precocious children who have carried on the sentimental business in all Mr. Dickens's novels; the Little Nells, the Smikes, the Paul Dombeys." [8] Yet despite the mawkish and morbid touches peculiar to them, Dickens's children serve as models of what the child figure's function in literature is: they are vehicles through which the question of man's fallen state is discussed, and their appearance brings with it a heavy supposition that the issue will be decided in favor of the view held by Augustine and the Church after him. When James himself came to use the child figure in *The Turn of the Screw* (1898), he disposed of what was mawkish in Dickens's children, but Miles and Flora pose the same questions—and force us to very much the same conclusions—as do Little Nell, Paul Dombey, and Jenny Wren; they are, in their own right, little monsters.

Of course, whether Miles and Flora are literally little monsters—"deformed, unhealthy, unnatural"—will depend on how the story is analyzed. The very name Flora, taken from the pages of Dickens himself and other sentimental authors of the era; the introduction which announces that the story is an exercise in which the storyteller "turns the screw"; the use of the governess character, so overworked in Victorian fiction; and the introduction of the supernatural—hardly James's first interest—all would seem to indicate that the story belongs with *Northanger Abbey* as a parody which transcends itself, a joke that was so good no one laughed. The central feature of the joke is the ambiguity which marks the whole production, and of course to be successful it must remain unresolved: is the story serious or not? is the governess an hysteric or can we believe her? are the children fiends or angels? If the story answered any of these questions, its power would be gone; the screw would no longer turn. Much criticism has been written to demonstrate that James intended one interpretation or another, which is to miss the goodness of the joke in *The Turn of the Screw*.[9] The point is that the ambiguity cannot be resolved in the story any more than it can in life, that we live with a perpetual ambiguity which, for want of clarification, we should at least savor and enjoy as we do a good story.

The ambiguity of the story resonates between two points, the sanity or credibility of the governess and the goodness, or lack of it, of the children. Ultimately, the two problems are the same. If the governess is mad, the children are as good as they seem; if the governess is in her right mind, the children are thoroughly corrupt. But either way, the world of Bly is invested with monumental evil, an evil in which the death of Miles is either the climax or catharsis. Whether Miles's death is the triumph *over* or the triumph *of* the powers of darkness, the essential point has been made that Bly is a fallen world throughout the course of the story, and as in Dickens, the contrast between the fallen and redeemed worlds is made by way of the child figures. "What do you say to *two* children—?" says the host on the first page of the story, approaching the whole situation with the glee of a technician who has discovered a powerful new tool.

What Dickens accomplished by sentiment, James does by ambiguity. Otherwise, the use of the child figure in each author is similar; Miles and Flora invite us to consider the question of man's original nature and his hope of redemption, and though their own goodness or corruption is a question in dispute, no matter which alternative we choose, we are forced to Augustine's conclusion that the world is a fallen place inhabited by fallen men.

Not every author, however, succumbed to the Augustinian use of the child figure with Dickens's enthusiastic conviction or James's ironic relish; some, in fact—often professed admirers of Wordsworth—believed that the child had a sweeter, more Pelagian role to play than anyone since Wordsworth himself had allowed it. Florian Deleal of Walter Pater's *The Child in the House* (1878) has a sensibility and significance very much like the child of *The Prelude;* for both, "all the acts and accidents of daily life borrowed a sacred colour and significance,"[10] though Florian is a house-reared child and precociously full of the high Anglican piety associated with the Oxford Movement—one pictures him as a pale, brooding creature, in contrast to the lively young savage of Wordsworth's *Prelude.* The children of Charles Kingsley's books often imitate the exuberance of Wordsworth's childhood portraits, but they never manage to capture their inner, transcendent joy. Numerous children's authors incorporated one aspect or another of Wordsworth's picture of childhood, but none duplicated the complete Wordsworthian synthesis of child, adult, and nature, and these authors are now largely forgotten.

But in George Eliot we have an author who professes Wordsworth's notion of childhood (but what would Wordsworth have thought of *Silas Marner?*) and has left an enduring novel which seeks to embody it. *Silas Marner* (1861) is prefaced by three lines from Wordsworth's "Michael" (1800):

> A child, more than all other gifts
> That earth can offer to declining man,
> Brings hope with it, and forward-looking thoughts.

Writing her publisher while *Silas Marner* was in progress, she guessed that no one would take an interest in the book, "since Wordsworth is dead."[11] Of course, it is hard to know if George Eliot meant the Wordsworth of *The Prelude,* the "Ode," or *Ecclesiastical Sonnets*—or whether she made a distinction. The presumption is that she was thinking of the early Wordsworth. Yet the child figure who emerges from *Silas Marner* bears only the most superficial resemblance to her counterparts in early Wordsworth. In fact, Eppie is strikingly similar to Dickens's children.

In *Silas Marner,* as in *The Old Curiosity Shop, Oliver Twist, Dombey and Son, A Christmas Carol,* and *Our Mutual Friend,* the child is intimately related to the figure of the old man or Old Adam, in this case, Silas himself. Silas's age is only apparent in the second half of the novel where the process of redemption and understanding set in motion by the appearance of the child figure is completed. In the final chapters, he is, like Scrooge or Riah, white-haired, bent, but possessing "a longer vision" (16). In the early part of the book, however, his connection with the Old Adam is abundantly clear. He belongs to an ultra-Calvinist religious sect in which Assurance of Salvation is much discussed but amounts to little more than "hope mingled with fear" (1). The village to which he comes, Raveloe, is peopled by "brawny country-folk," who "looked like the remnants of a disinherited race" (1). Silas's trade, weaving, is connected by the author and the village people with "the Evil One" (1), while classical analogy suggests the connection between weaving and the three Fates, inexorably spinning out the thread of life in very much the same way that Silas's Calvinist deity has from eternity ordained the disposition of souls and time itself. Silas's spinning, in conjunction with his perpetual condemnation by his fellow Dissenters, allows him to amass a horde of gold in seclusion, which he enjoys not as a means to any end, but as an end in itself. Like the old man of Chaucer's Pardoner's Tale, Silas is linked to a cache of gold (the *radix malorum* of Chaucer's story) which leads to the death of a greedy young man. Even when Silas is not yet forty, "the children always called him 'Old Master Marner'" (2) and the villagers, when he appears in the tavern, mistake him for an apparition.

If there is anything in George Eliot's portrait of the Old Adam not found in Dickens, it is that where Dickens had emphasized the connection of the old man with the Old Law by making Fagin and Riah Jews, George Eliot makes her old man a Calvinist. This allows her to associate the Calvinist conceptions of Election and Salvation with the bondage of the Old Adam; here, the theory of God's foreknowledge and foredooming of human souls is not a consequence, but an aspect of Original Sin. This modest plea for a benign view of free will is the closest *Silas*

*Marner* comes to Wordsworth's early philosophy, however; Eppie is otherwise modeled according to the traditional use of the child figure, as Silas had been according
to the traditional *vetus homo.*

Eppie's substitution for Silas's lost gold, her appearance
during the Christmas season on New Year's Eve, and
her birth through the process of sin and degradation which
Silas himself represents—all these place the child firmly
within the boundaries of Christian imagery. But *Silas
Marner* is not a book that draws its literary figures or
makes its points by halves; after this bold introduction of
the child, another scene follows in which the theological
import of the figure is spelled out. Silas is urged to have
Eppie christened.

> Dolly's word "christened" conveyed no distinct mean-
> ing to him. He had only heard of baptism, and had
> only seen the baptism of grown men and women.
> "What is it as you mean by 'christened'?" he said
> at last, timidly. "Won't folks be good to her without
> it?"
> "Dear, dear! Master Marner," said Dolly, with gentle
> distress and compassion. "Had you never no father nor
> mother as taught you to say your prayers, and as
> there's good words and good things to keep us from
> harm?"
> "Yes," said Silas, in a low voice; "I know a deal
> about that—used to, used to. But your ways are differ-
> ent: my country was a good way off."     (14)

Silas has only heard of baptism; christening, with its
implied significance of Christ's universal salvation, is
foreign to him. His memory of "good words and good
things" is indistinct, and he readily admits that he comes
from a land "a good way off," the world of the Old
Covenant where Christ's redemption is unknown.

Eppie is duly christened, and her christening is the
means of Silas's reintroduction into the community in
which he lives. This new interest in turn reawakens his
enthusiasm for the natural world:

> He had no distinct idea about the baptism and the
> church-going, except that Dolly had said it was for the
> good of the child; and in this way, as the weeks grew
> to months, the child created fresh and fresh links be-
> tween his life and the lives from which he had hitherto
> shrunk continually into narrower isolation. Unlike the
> gold which needed nothing, and must be worshipped in
> close-locked solitude—which was hidden away from the
> daylight, was deaf to the song of birds, and started to
> no human tones—Eppie was a creature of endless claims
> and ever-growing desires, seeking and loving sunshine
> . . . and warming him into joy because *she* had joy. (14)

There is a strong dose of Rousseau and Wordsworth in
these last phrases, which imply a spontaneous and transcendent adult joy in the created universe captured
through the perception of childhood, but here the joy
stems not simply from the child, but from the ritual
and process associated with the child. Eppie's baptism
is literally and figuratively a new start for Silas; it is from
that redemptive moment that he reintegrates himself into
humanity and gradually gains an appreciation for nature.

If *Silas Marner* is based on Wordsworth's vision of
childhood, it is either based on the late Wordsworth or
on a misconception of his early vision. *Silas Marner* is a
book full of Augustinian dogma and with few immediate
joys. What joys there are come not so much in the present
moment or in transcendence but through the ability of
childhood to lead us through Apocalypse to Paradise:
"In old days there were angels who came and took men

by the hand and led them away from the city of destruction. We see no white-winged angels now. But yet men are led away from threatening destruction: a hand is put into theirs, which leads them forth gently towards a calm and bright land, so that they look no more backward; and the hand may be a little child's" (14). Even the time structure of *Silas Marner* belies any trace of Wordsworth: the novel is both a history and a parable—it is written in biblical time, occurring both in one specific period and in all periods simultaneously. Wordsworth, on the other hand, is content to feel and experience within one lifetime of sensation; whatever intimations he has are defined and circumscribed by the historical span into which he was born. But *Silas Marner* is still coherent if we imagine it taking place in a higher time scheme, simultaneous with the destruction of the Cities of the Plain, as the quotation above suggests we do, or whether we are content that the time of the book falls between the French Revolution and the pre–Reform Bill agitation. This biblical time scheme is naturally suited to the presentation of the figures of the child and old man, as well as the discussion of those themes which accompany their presentation. It is, however, not particularly fitted to the genial spontaneity of early Wordsworth.

It is possible that George Eliot equated Wordsworth's philosophy with a love of pastoral scenery; after the publication of *Silas Marner,* in a letter to her publisher about the book's reception, she mentions her contempt for the prospect of crowded cities "less and less under the influence of Nature—i.e., the sky, the hills and the plains."[12] But even St. Augustine might enjoy the sky, hills, and plains without remorse—this is not the love of nature

Blake found tantamount to devil worship. The devil enters in when the individual, in his rapport with nature, believes he has found sufficiency and highest truth. Wordsworth's early visions of childhood depict exactly this belief, and to Blake this was nothing more than the worship of our own fallen nature and the image of it impressed upon a fallen world. But *Silas Marner,* for all that it is set among hill, sky, and plain, does not depict Wordsworth's nature; here as in Dickens, the child is a contrast to the fallen world and the means of its redemption.

If George Eliot does approach Wordsworth's conception of childhood, it is in *The Mill on the Floss* (1860). The child Eppie is clearly a literary figure, drawn not so much from life as to make a point about it. But in Tom and Maggie Tulliver, George Eliot gives minutely detailed and psychological character studies which are simultaneously from and about life. This scheme of characterization is compatible both with the early Wordsworth's insistence on immanence and rational philosophy's concern with the observation of cause and effect: "Does not science tell us that its highest striving is after the ascertainment of a unity which shall bind the smallest things with the greatest?" George Eliot asks in *The Mill on the Floss* (4.1). Answering her own question, she replies, "It is surely the same with the observation of human life." So far at least, Wordsworth and the rationalist philosophy to which George Eliot was devoted are engaged in a common pursuit, "the ascertainment of a unity" within the boundaries of felt and observable life.

This curious point of alliance between Wordsworth and rationalist philosophy deserves closer attention because it sheds light on nineteenth-century views of the child as well as on the childhood portraits of *The Mill on the Floss*. Childhood held a certain fascination for the rationalists precisely because it could be observed; surely cause and effect were at work here, if one only had the key. John Stuart Mill remarked that his science of ethology (a means of deducing the constituents of character—we would call it an aspect of psychology) properly began with the observation of childhood: "It would be necessary to know and record every sensation or impression received by the young pupil from a period long before it could speak, including its own notions respecting the sources of all those sensations and impressions."[13] This challenge intrigued the scientific mind of the period far more than the poetic; Coleridge, in condemning several implications of Wordsworth's "Ode," had written that it was futile to try reading the child mind—if such a thing could be said to exist at all: "In what sense is a child of that age a '*Philosopher*'? In what sense does he *read* 'the eternal deep'? . . . These would be tidings indeed. . . . Children at this age give us no such information of themselves; and at what time were we dipped in the Lethe, which has produced such utter oblivion of a state so godlike?"[14]

But like Wordsworth, the rationalists were prepared at least to consider the observation and understanding of the child mind. Mill himself, with his fellow meliorist George Eliot, was a great admirer of Wordsworth—partially, like her, because Wordsworth was the poet of sky, hill, and plain (Mill calls them "rural objects and natural scenery"[15]), but more importantly because his poetry appeared to be compatible with Mill's scientific outlook—he could at once be read as a meliorist poet writing of the shared stuff of physical sensations: "In them [Wordsworth's poems] I seemed to draw from a source of inward joy, of sympathetic and imaginative pleasure, which could be shared by all human beings; which had no connexion with struggle or imperfection, but would be made richer by every improvement in the physical or social condition of mankind."[16] With this supposedly mutual climate of opinion, it is not surprising to find Mill or George Eliot pursuing what they considered to be Wordsworth's vision of childhood: if childhood, as Mill had hoped, could be observed in its "sensations and impressions," this knowledge would aid immeasurably in the creation of that ameliorated world which the rationalists were in the process of building.

Something of this ambition lies behind the childhood studies in *The Mill on the Floss*. Speaking of the lack of grandeur and vision in her choice of characters and setting, George Eliot justifies herself by saying, "I share with you this sense of oppressive narrowness; but it is necessary that we should feel it, if we care to understand how it acted on the lives of Tom and Maggie—how it has acted on young natures in many generations, that in the onward tendency of human things have risen above the mental level of the generation before them, to which they have been nevertheless tied by the strongest fibres of their hearts" (4.1). In other words, a full understanding of the children Tom and Maggie is necessary to appreciate the delicate mechanism by which humanity marches forward.

Yet, amid these Pelagian sentiments of man's perfectibility, the rationalists maintain an Augustinian strain which vitiates a good deal of their similarity to Wordsworth. Wordsworth, after all, had not been a meliorist; he had believed in the perfection of the present moment, not perfectibility of the future. With him, the child embodied the joy available to anyone, at any time, through rapport with themselves and nature. This is not the same nature of which Mill says, "the ways of Nature are to be conquered, not obeyed."[17] In the same essay, Mill goes on to speak of nature as on a footing with the common criminal and asserts that "the duty of man is the same in respect to his own nature as in respect to the nature of all other things, namely not to follow but to amend it."[18] While he clings to the Pelagian notion that man is capable of redeeming himself without assistance, his portrait of nature is consistent with the dogmatic view of fallen man in a fallen universe.

The uneasy alliance of Pelagian meliorism and an Augustinian universe occurs in *The Mill on the Floss* and helps explain the divergence between the first and second halves of the novel. The first half is full of careful observation of childhood; it captures the energy, as well as the egotism and charm, of the vision of childhood in *The Prelude*. Like Wordsworth's portrait of himself in youth, Maggie is not without fears, doubts, and emotions, and she has the same self-enclosed power and delight: "Maggie always looked at Lucy with delight. She was fond of fancying a world where the people never got any larger than children of their own age, and she made the queen of it just like Lucy, with a little crown on her head, and a little sceptre in her hand . . . only the queen was Maggie herself in Lucy's form" (1.7). This exuberant egoism illuminates the first part of *The Mill on the Floss,* but the second half looks for no way to recapture and harness it, as Wordsworth had in his "Ode." Instead, with the close of Tom and Maggie's childhood comes the realization that "they had gone forth together into their new life of sorrow, and they would never more see the sunshine undimmed by remembered cares. They had entered the thorny wilderness, and the golden gates of childhood had for ever closed behind them" (2.7). This backward look at childhood not only recalls the final lines of *Paradise Lost,* but the dogmatic scheme behind *Paradise Lost.* Whatever the Wordsworthian charms of childhood here, it is not possible to sustain them in fallen adulthood or fallen nature. The river and Tom's and Maggie's passions demonstrate the impossibility.

If *The Mill on the Floss* begins in Wordsworth's world of innate childhood pleasures, it ends in the universe of Original Sin which had been the milieu of *Silas Marner.* There, the child had appeared at the middle of the novel to redeem age; in *The Mill on the Floss* the pattern is reversed: age comes midway to destroy childish joys. The debt to Wordsworth, more apparent than real in *Silas Marner* and more real than apparent in *The Mill on the Floss,* is in neither novel sufficient to overcome the inherent attraction of the child figure for the Christian doctrines of sin and redemption, even if George Eliot had wished to separate the two.

In the end, the same attraction overwhelmed the rationalists' theories of childhood. Undoubtedly, the challenge of finding a scientific, cause-and-effect relationship between child and adult, as Wordsworth had done poetically in the "Ode," stimulated observation of children and speculation about that childhood condition of mind which Coleridge had dismissed as a Lethean unknown. As early as 1840, Darwin wrote his "Biographical Sketch of an Infant," and by 1877 George Henry Lewes published his

"Consciousness and Unconsciousness,"[19] an article very modern in tone which attempts to chart the region which Freud later identified as the common ground of childhood memory and adult behavior. But the more that early childhood was investigated, the harder it seemed to maintain Mill's synthesis of perfectible man and degenerate nature. An unnamed reviewer for the Anglo-Catholic *British Critic* had attacked Mill's *System of Logic* as a species of heresy because of this synthesis: "If Mr. Mill's principles be adopted as a full statement of truth, the whole fabric of Christian theology must totter and fall. . . . Man, left to his own nature, acts on laws, which may be calculated and made the subject of a science: granted; yet that he was left to his own nature was a punishment for sin; the laws on which he acts are habits of sin; and that any individual does act on them exclusively is in his case an instance of sin."[20] By the end of the century, and even more so at the end of World War I, this view had won out, not because it was good religion, but because it seemed to make good sense. As George Santayana said of the fifth century, "It was hardly necessary to preach the doctrine of Original Sin to that society; the visible blight that had fallen on classic civilization was proof enough of that."[21] The world in which Hardy wrote and Tennyson completed his *Idylls of the King,* a world whose chief artistic movement was styled Decadent, required little persuasion to believe that man and nature had fallen together. When Freud finally met the challenge of explaining the cause-and-effect mechanisms of childhood by propounding a theory which appeared to be nothing more than a quasi-scientific rendition of Augustine's Original Sin arguments, the British accepted it with only minor opposition—certainly without the furor Darwin had caused only sixty years earlier.

*The Mill on the Floss* and *Silas Marner*, through their child figures, partake of the debate that occurred within the rationalist and scientific communities as to whether it was possible to have a fallen universe with an unfallen man in residence, and they reflect the outcome of that debate by reaching the conclusion that it is not.

# V

# Through the Child's Eyes: Gosse, Dickens, and Henry James

"Quis me commemorat peccatum infantiae meae, quoniam nemo mundus a peccato coram te?" asks Augustine in his *Confessions* (1.7). "Who can summon to my remembrance the sins of my childhood—for no man is sinless in Thy sight?" The *Confessions* itself replies to the saint's question: each man is obliged to recall his own sins and expose them, at least to himself. The religious and intellectual debates already outlined here, which gave rise to the child figure in literature, also stimulated an introspective and confessional attitude which finds an outlet in autobiography and first-person narratives in general, and there is nothing accidental in the virtually simultaneous appearance of the child as an object of theological dispute and the autobiographical genre, nor in the fact that both these currents meet in the works of St. Augustine.

Although several critics have tried to demonstrate the existence of an autobiographical genre before Augustine, they are generally forced to accept the *Confessions* as the first example of the "modern type"[1] or to define the genre so loosely that it ceases to exist. Georg Misch, for instance, calls autobiography "a representation of life that is committed to no definite form"[2] and Wayne Shumaker

makes an attempt to establish a classical variety of autobiography to include Socrates' defense in the *Apology* and
Caesar's *Commentaries,* though the first is as much Plato's
as Socrates' and the second avoids self-revelation by using
the third person. Shumaker, however, rapidly moves away
from this contention and speaks instead of "the development of an assumption that the lives of individual persons
were important *in themselves,* whether or not they would
be regarded as exemplary,"[3] of which type of writing
Augustine is the model. This definition, however, does not
go far enough: it might explain the motives of Plutarch
as well as George Fox. The autobiographical impulse from
its appearance in Augustine to the present seems necessarily to contain the idea of confession and hence of guilt.

Of course, here as before an exception has to be made
for Rousseau and Wordsworth. Like their visions of childhood, Rousseau's *Confessions* and Wordsworth's *Prelude*
are written—perhaps purposely—in contradiction to the
Augustinian notion of confession as a necessary aspect
of universal guilt. Once again, in their concentration on
the unassisted powers and joys of individual life, Rousseau
and Wordsworth cast themselves in the Pelagian role. But
what generally separates Plutarch from George Fox is not
simply the assumption that individual lives are important,
exemplary or not, but the belief which is common in
autobiography from Augustine onward that the importance of the individual is a function of the role he, as a
fallen man, plays in a fallen world.

Such a view naturally involves the idea of confession,
and Augustine's thoroughness in self-revelation is a model
for this type of literary expression unrivalled to this day.
Autobiography, however, need not take such an extreme

form, and may, in fact, be rather unpenitent. The essential ingredients are that the individual be recognized as important in and of himself; that he acknowledge his imperfection; and that he understand his imperfection as part of a larger, imperfect universe. Hence Trollope's *Autobiography* succeeds today, and shocked in his own, not because of its penitence, but because of its candid admissions of monetary gain and an artistry so business-like as to seem callous. The author's personal acknowledgment of guilt is unimportant so long as his audience finds all the ingredients of a confession present. Even an author as remote from Augustine as John Stuart Mill makes a success of his *Autobiography* at the moment he recalls the collapse of his perfectly fashioned Benthamite universe and the realization of his intellectual imperfection. Gibbon's *Autobiography* stands out as an exception to the Christian, Augustinian tradition, an exception, if not premeditated, at least in keeping with the temper of the man.

The child figure, whose presence in literature is so deeply rooted in the concepts of a fallen world and man's guilt, occupies a great deal of common ground with autobiography: the child in literature reveals. Whether an author takes the position of Augustine that the child reveals the wickedness of this world in his own corruption of will or Dickens's modified attitude that the child figure is an innocent foil to the depravity of the universe, revealing by the contrast he makes, the child's role is to expose the essential imperfections of the world around him. Autobiography and first-person narratives (especially those written from the perspective of childhood) serve much the same purpose. In Augustine, this function is clear and simple: a description of childhood will be a portrait of sin, virtually in its original condition, for the child is a sinner "unius diei vita super terram" (1.7), at one day old. In the works discussed below, the child is not so much a sinner as the means by which guilt is ferreted out and understood to be pervasive. The alteration, then, is one of method and not intent, though with Freudian analysis, the child once again became both the perpetrator and prosecutor of guilt.

The development of Freud's theory of infantile sexuality is a striking example of the connection between the autobiographical impulse and the child figure. It was Freud's own self-analysis which confirmed his notion of the link between dream, guilt, and instinctive childhood desire (Augustine would have preferred "will" for "desire" or "id"). In Freud's examination of his own childhood and the technique of psychoanalysis which grows out of his theory, the analyst at once detaches himself from his own life sufficiently to have a critical point of view and at the same time involves himself so completely in his recollections that the material for evaluation is presented fresh and entire. The result is a body of childhood fantasies, desires, and dreams controlled and explained by a mature, dominating critical faculty. The same technique is commonly used in the autobiographical style, whether in fiction or nonfiction: a mature, tempered narrator casts himself back into his past, at once reliving and explaining it. In Freud's case the result was, in Ernest Jones's words, the "assertion that children are born with sexual urges, which undergo a complicated development before they attain the familiar adult form, and that their first sexual objects are their parents."[4] In his discovery Freud felt he had solved the riddle of the sphinx. The autobiographical genre similarly reveals and exposes, usually with the same challenge to innocency contained in the Freudian assertion. In this, autobiography is very unlike biography, which has traditionally aggrandized its subjects. When it cannot or does not choose to dignify its subjects, biography normally elevates them in some other way: Lytton Strachey's Queen Victoria emerges from his debunking not less grand, but simply grand in a different way.

Gosse's *Father and Son,* taken together with his biography of his father, *The Naturalist of the Sea-Shore,* highlights the distinction between biography and autobiography, the way in which autobiography reveals, and the role of the child in this process. *The Naturalist of the Sea-Shore* appeared in 1896, eleven years before *Father and Son.* It is the model of Victorian biography, and the Philip Gosse who emerges from its pages is a character more serene, more grand, and infinitely less interesting than the temperamental Father of the autobiographical sketch. The absurdities of *Father and Son* are deleted; there is no description of the monomaniacally Calvinist Father hasting the Christmas pudding from the servants' quarters and burying the "idolatrous confectionery" in the rubbish heap. Nor is the sense of failed love which makes the portrait of the father in the autobiographical study so complex and sympathetic conveyed in the standard biography.

On the other hand, much of the characterization of the father in the autobiography appears distorted or one-sided in light of the information in the biography, as if Gosse were consciously fashioning not an historical account, but a literary one. Facts and details from the biography are omitted or underplayed in the autobiography in order to make the figure of Philip Gosse more like a character in a novel and less like the equally curious individual he was; thus historical accuracy is subordinated to aesthetic judgment in order to produce a work which conveys a deeper significance than permitted by factual precision.

The Philip Gosse of *Father and Son* is a figure whose stern religion has biased every aspect of taste and conduct; his temperament has been permanently molded—or warped, depending on the perspective of the reader—by a single, overriding conviction. Even the father's admiration of Vergil is laid to the traditional Christian attitude toward classical authors that "he is the one who can be enjoyed with the least to explain away and least to excuse" (7). *The Naturalist of the Sea-Shore,* however, presents a father more rounded and distinctly more flexible in taste and behavior. From the earlier account, Philip Gosse was a great admirer of Wordsworth, took delight in Byron, and owned sets of the works of Walter Scott and Fielding. In *Father and Son,* Gosse tells how his father forbade him Scott's novels while permitting him to read his poetry. What he doesn't tell us, however, is that this scruple was as likely a literary as a moral one.

In fact, to judge from Philip Gosse's taste in poetry as outlined in *The Naturalist of the Sea-Shore,* the elder Gosse exhibited a surprisingly lively and modern critical approach: "He was much more interested, toward the end, in portions of Swinburne and Rossetti, than he had ever been in Tennyson and Browning, for whom he had the slightest tolerance," [5] his son tells us in the biography. He also mentions his father's lifelong fondness for Shelley. The Philip Gosse of this romantic literary persuasion is carefully expunged from *Father and Son,* leaving instead the portrait of a towering fanatic consumed only by his passion for an outmoded religious ideal.

From one point of view, then, *The Naturalist of the Sea-Shore* is the fuller and more accurate of the two books; yet *Father and Son* is not simply the more interesting account, but the one that rings true despite its omissions and distortions. The truth of the autobiographical study lies in its very subjectivity; in its willingness to sacrifice historical fact to the construction of a cohesive literary fable; and in the perspective with which the reader is provided—not that of an austere biographer but of an older man looking through the eyes of his childhood.

In *Father and Son,* as in Augustine's *Confessions,* a penitent man looks back through the eyes of a youth he considers to have been at odds with his present state of enlightenment, and the ever-present contrast of the two states gives the narrative its particular momentum and fervor. But in *Father and Son* the enlightenment is not one of religious zeal; it is rather one of a very secular nature, skeptical, amused, and indulgent. What had been wicked in Augustine is in Gosse absurd. Gosse pursues the absurd, as seen through the eyes of his childhood, with a fervor as dedicated as Augustine's and perhaps to the same ends.

*Father and Son,* called by its author "the record of a struggle between two temperaments, two consciences and almost two epochs" (1), is a study in duality. There is first the struggle between father and son, which, as in *Dombey and Son,* implies a larger conflict between the child god and his Old Covenant father. Second, the double nature of the child himself is an essential feature of the narrative; and finally, there is the dual perspective of the whole enterprise, the mature narrator looking through the eyes of childhood, from which the wit of the book grows.

*Father and Son* is, as Gosse wished it to be, the story of the struggle of two epochs. When the book was published in 1907, Philip Gosse and the style he represented were already regarded as curiosities of an age, however great, marked by a singular lack of humor and charm. The heroes of the new century were the men who had liberated society from the high seriousness of Carlyle, Gladstone, Tennyson, and Holman Hunt. Arthur Balfour, if not society's finest ornament, then perhaps the brightest man in England, was the light of the Conservative Party and English politics. Whistler and Sargent, Oscar Wilde and Henry James represented the modern taste in art and literature; Hardy, who might have threatened to perpetuate the tone of the preceding age, had given up the prose which tied him to high Victoriana. In this atmosphere, Gosse's autobiography was read, as it still is today, as a fable of liberation. If in *Dombey and Son* Dickens had transformed the patriarchal Old Testament father into a kindly, Sunday school grandfather, Gosse went him one better and simply turned his back on the old man. That the weapons by which he overcame were wit, candor, and irony perfectly suited the temper of the new generation.

In *Dombey and Son* the child presides over a rearrangement of Christian myth to Dickens's specifications. In Gosse, the child is hero precisely because he dismantles the whole mythic structure the father represents and then walks away from it. Like Paul, the figure of young Gosse is an infant god come as a champion of the new order, but here he is a secular god whose kingdom is very much of this earth.

For Dickens, the Bible had been a source, and its presence is felt throughout his work. In Gosse, the biblical echo is still heard, but as a means of wit, almost of parody, a counterpoint against the new secular style: "I could not fail to be aware of the fact that literature tempted me to stray up innumerable paths which meandered in directions at right angles to that direct straight way which leadeth to salvation" (12). The sense of this passage and its style are in complete harmony; the profession of literature is irreconcilable with the father's religion, and the secular calling naturally leads to a parody of the religious style. That parody is extended to the names Father and Son in the text, which by their capitalization emphasize the way in which Gosse turns the religious myth against itself; the son has come to save the world from the father's religion.

The mechanics of this salvation involve the double outlook of the Son as depicted by Gosse, for just as there is a mature narrator looking at the world with a child's eyes in his autobiography, the child himself plays a dual role which enables him to put his father's world in the perspective of wit and eventually overcome it:

> I had found a companion and a confidant in myself.
> There was a secret in this world and it belonged to me
> and to a somebody who lived in the same body with
> me. There were two of us, and we could talk with
> one another. It is difficult to define impressions so rudi-
> mentary, but it is certain that it was in this dual form
> that the sense of my individuality now suddenly de-
> scended upon me.                                    (2)

Gosse's awareness of a second self comes when he realizes his father is not "omniscient or infallible"; and while one self continues to pose as the model child, obedient to his father, this second self begins a catalogue of his father's fallibility which ends not so much with the break that comes at the end of the story as with the writing of the autobiography over fifty years later.

This second self necessarily makes the character of the son more attractive than the father, for the Son, even when being a pious fraud, is always dynamic, while the father is static in outlook and belief. When the son, at the age of eleven, is baptized into the Plymouth Brethren, he goes through the motions with perfect piety. But the second self, whose function it is to record the follies of the world around him, cannot stand idly by during this pageant. For him, the font "might have been supposed to be a swimming-bath"; the lady who miraculously falls into the pool and becomes an object of wonder to the congregation is an object of mirth to Gosse's double; the other candidates for baptism are "the humdrum adults who followed in my wet and glorious footsteps." At the end of the service he records "that some of the other little boys presently complained to Mary Grace that I put out my tongue at them in mockery . . . to remind them that I now broke bread as one of the Saints, and that they did not" (8). This proud, condescending alter ego observes the world around him and does not hesitate to stick out his tongue. From his observations *Father and Son* gets its wit, and in his eventual renunciation of both the father and the yielding son whose body he inhabits, the book acquires a hero.

The split between the young Gosse who faithfully plays out the role ordained by his father and the second self who shares his body, observing and reinterpreting each performance, is reflected in the narration of the story itself. Gosse the raconteur, librarian of the House of Lords, friend of Swinburne, Hardy, and James, controls the flow of the story. He puts events in chronological order, tactfully changes the names of the participants, and gives the narrative direction in much the same way the analyst reconstructs childhood recollections to make them intelligible to adult logic. But the raw material with which this mature narrator works is the product of the alter ego whose triumphant emergence is the focus of the book. In collaboration, these two narrators make the book at once realistic and ludicrous. Had the story been written strictly from a mature point of view, the result might resemble the work of Mark Rutherford; had it been done solely from the perspective of the child's alter ego, it might have read like Lewis Carroll. The combination of views has the realism of the first author and the sense of having arrived at a deeper insight found in the second: the child's perspective has a priority in truthfulness which defeats the gravity of adult life while at the same time raising grave questions about the network of venalities which pass for maturity, and the adult's point of view gives the book a coherence which makes it intelligible to the adult world it depicts.

The child's ability to perceive the true nature of the world around him is conceded both in Christian dogma and the romanticism of Rousseau and Wordsworth, though for very different reasons. For Wordsworth, of course, the child is all the closer to "that imperial palace whence he came"; his perception is not yet blinded by "the light of common day." For Augustine, however, and Christian orthodoxy after him, the child is indeed closer to an original source: in him, Adam's sin is distilled to its purest form. The child, without the wit to disguise sin or the strength to indulge it, represents man's fallen condition in its most essential manifestation. Also, the child of Christian theology has a better claim on truthfulness by virtue of his baptism, a custom so universal in the centuries following Augustine that the need to mention it has passed out of conscious thought; hence we refer to a person's Christian name, meaning the name given in baptism, regardless of whether he has in fact been baptized or even whether he is a Christian. Not only is the child closer to the essence of sin, he is in this view nearer to the expiation of it. In both senses, he is nearer the unsullied truth than an adult, a position developed and reinforced by Freud, whose picture of the child as pure id without the encumbrances of a superego and its consequence, guilt, is a modification of, but hardly a challenge to, the position developed by the Church.

If, however, the child's point of view carries more weight, it is still a child's view. It is necessarily more unrefined and underveloped than an adult's, qualities which at once enhance its truthfulness and undermine its logic. Works like *Father and Son* which rest so heavily on the child's viewpoint naturally take on aspects of absurdity, as well as of the literary mode of absurdism.

Here, in relation to the child figure, the term *absurd* is used to mean the depiction of a venal universe without overt moral condemnation and with an honest, child-like simplicity which to the adult audience seems illogical or perverse by reason of the audience's own corruption. Hence, by this definition, the perfect absurdist work would seem fully logical and realistic to the perfect man. Of course, this notion of the absurd has behind it the very moral idea that to show the world through the eyes of a child, honestly and simply, is to reveal the follies of a fallen universe. In *Father and Son,* for instance, the young Gosse tests his father's warnings against idolatry by a simple experiment:

> I was in the morning-room on the ground-floor, where, with much labour, I hoisted a small chair on to the table close to the window. My heart was now beating as if it would leap out of my side, but I pursued my experiment. I knelt down on the carpet in front of the table and looking up I said my daily prayer in a loud voice, only substituting the address "O Chair!" for the habitual one.
>
> Having carried this act of idolatry safely through, I waited to see what would happen. It was a fine day. . . . But nothing happened; there was not a cloud in the sky, not an unusual sound in the street. Presently I was quite sure that nothing would happen. I had committed idolatry, flagrantly and deliberately, and God did not care.                                    (2)

This perfectly absurd scene (it is reminiscent of Alice's decision to address the Mouse in the vocative case as "O Mouse!") is meant, with a minimum of judgment and the maximum of directness, to establish that the father's excessive dogmatism itself partakes of a fallen universe. The father's religion, like Silas Marner's before the advent of Eppie, is a species of the sin it continually decries, and here the child very simply points out that as such, it is not so much wrong as absurd.

*Father and Son* owes much of its potency to its use of the absurd. While it is often a story about morality, it is almost never a moral narrative. Gosse merely places himself inside the framework of his childhood recollections and observes. The resulting narration is free of judgments, and the sequence of events, as well as the events themselves, are marked by the same illogic encountered in daily life. In chapter 10, for instance, where the father takes his son aside and tells him of his impending remarriage, the scene that follows is distinguished by its illogic: "A new mamma was coming; I was sure to like her. Still in a non-committal mood, I asked: 'Will she go with me to the back of the lime-kiln?'" This is the father's first defeat in his attempt to make his impending marriage fit his own scheme of order and propriety, but certainly not his last. The son proceeds to guess that the prospective bride is "a married woman who kept a sweet-shop in the village," and then, after learning who she in fact will be, cross-examines his father on her religious principles. "Our positions were now curiously changed. It seemed as if it were I who was the jealous monitor, and my Father the deprecating penitent. I sat up in the coverlid, and I shook a finger at him. 'Papa,' I said, 'don't tell me that she's a pedobaptist?'"

The ease with which the son is able to stand the father's highly developed system of values on its head deflates it more efficiently and rapidly than any reasoned argument could; the child observes that the father's system is absurd, and the narration through his eyes demonstrates it to be so. The young Gosse surveys the world around him like the messiah of a new covenant exposing the frauds of the Old Law, and the method of exposing these frauds is simply to observe with the eyes of a child and let the results speak for themselves.

*David Copperfield* (1849–1850), which, if not Dickens's autobiography, is at least as accurate a portrait of his childhood as *Father and Son* is of Gosse's, gives a similarly absurd picture of adult life. In chapter 11, Dickens describes the absurdist effect obtained by looking at the world through the eyes of a child: "When I tread the old ground, I do not wonder that I seem to see and pity, going on before me, an innocent romantic boy, making his imaginative world out of such strange experiences and sordid things." In *David Copperfield,* an "imaginative world," in which judgments are not made, substitutes for "the strange experiences and sordid things" which are the common fare of Dickens's novels. And David's first-person narration, which even in adulthood never loses the perspective of childhood, is the means by which Dickens accomplishes this shift away from his usually invective style toward an equally moral, but unmoralizing, "imaginative" vision.

*David Copperfield* is unique among Dickens's novels in several respects. Dickens himself calls the book his favorite in the preface to the 1869 edition of his work. *David Copperfield* is also one of Dickens's two books in the autobiographical style, *Great Expectations* being the other. But while Pip is very much like David—what is true of the young David generally applies as well to the young Pip—*Great Expectations* is a book about growing up; *David Copperfield* is a story about never growing up. With *Father and Son, David Copperfield* looks at adult life through the eyes of childhood and rejects it as an alternative; the charm of Gosse's self-portrait and Dickens's David lies in their ability to retain the qualities that mark their childhoods even as they reach maturity. Dickens, again in the preface of 1869, speaks of David as "a favorite child," and although half the novel deals with the hero's adult life, Dickens succeeds in making of David an eternal juvenile.

Perhaps it is this sense of seeing with the vision of perpetual youth which makes *David Copperfield* the most congenial of Dickens's books outside of *The Pickwick Papers*. Compare, for instance, the death of Jo in *Bleak House,* accompanied as it is by the narrator's dithyrambic tirade, with David's cool and limpid account of his mother's death, which as surely as Jo's had been hastened by evil agents. First, David described the funeral parlor, "where we found three young women at work on a quantity of black materials, which were heaped upon the table, and little bits and cuttings of which were littered all over the floor" (9). The three women at their sewing in the undertaker's parlor recall the three Fates. Touches like this in David's narrative stress the imaginative quality of the whole. They indicate without the necessity of the author's intrusion. Mr. Sowerberry's funeral parlor in *Oliver Twist* is, as the reader is told in so many words, "tainted with the smell of coffins" (5). Speaking for himself, Dickens is forced to make the scene there grotesque; it frightens us in the same way the horrors of the fun house do. But by simply observing detail through David's eyes, *David Copperfield* becomes full of vivid imaginative elements. The funeral parlor David describes is no amusement-park terror, but genuinely chilling—it is the home of the Fates.

But the book is also unique in its lack of moral invective. Where *Dombey and Son,* which preceded it, and *Bleak House,* which followed, are full of the flavor of a jeremiad, *David Copperfield* looks at the world more in sorrow than anger. Forster described this quality of the novel by saying that "in the use of humour to bring out predominantly the ludicrous in any object or incident without excluding or weakening its most enchanting sentiment, it stands decidedly first [among Dickens's work]." [6] What Edmund Wilson describes as the "idealized" [7] nature of *David Copperfield* is precisely its absence of ethical judgment, its preference for ridicule over satire. This quality certainly alters the usual Dickensian mood, softening the rage, but does nothing to effect the sorrowful and disturbing atmosphere which normally surrounds the visible world in Dickens. Even Mr. Micawber, whose character is the triumph of the ludicrous over the outraged, has in his name a homophone of "macabre." Dickens's ludicrous world of childhood vision is no less fallen and perverse than the dark vision of his later novels.

The moral rage which is so prominent a part of Dickens's major novels—the portraits of violence and human mutilation through which that rage expressed itself—are gone from David's narrative. Steerforth alone among the book's characters receives the capital stroke Dickens so generously meted out elsewhere, and even Steerforth's death, placed beside the ghastly demise of Carker of Mr. Tulkinghorn, looks like an act of kindness; it is treated with pity rather than the relish Dickens could so easily muster for these occasions. Within the framework of *David Copperfield,* however, Steerforth's crime as well as his punishment is of the highest order: he has, as one critic says, "that secular semblance of grace, called charm"; [8] but beyond the fault of impersonating a gentleman, about which Dickens felt so strongly, he does what David never permits himself to do—he grows up to behave like the adults David has observed through the supercritical lens of childhood. He dies less because he is a cad than because he grows up. His death is indicative of the fate which awaits those who threaten the citadel of childhood vision.

But while Steerforth demonstrates the inadvisability of becoming an adult, Dora, the "child-bride," who dies within pages of Steerforth, illustrates the impossibility of remaining one type of eternal juvenile. David is obliged to sail between the Scylla and Charybdis represented by Steerforth and Dora, and he does. In the end, he obtains a state in which he leads the life of an adult with the spirit of a child, which in Dickens is as special a grace as baptism is in the church.

*David Copperfield* is, of all Dickens's work, the one which has enjoyed a continuous and high critical reputation. It is, like a fairy tale, almost beyond criticism—so much so that the title has almost become synonymous with literature itself. Undoubtedly, much of the book's vitality comes from Dickens's intense personal involvement with the story and much of its critical success stems from the use Proust and post-Freudian authors have made of it. But beyond these, *David Copperfield* combines two seeming opposites into a whole which seems to be irresistible: it is at once the high-water mark of realism, a book which, through its child narrator, presents a picture of life which is exact in its detail and unflawed by the sense that an authorial point of view is coloring the narration—in short, a thoroughly convincing portrait of things as they are. At the same time, the book has all the qualities of a children's story; it follows its own logic;

it looks at the world of adults as an absurdist spectacle, just as children are accustomed to see it in nursery rhymes; it indulges that most cherished fantasy, that of never growing up, to the point of triumph. David does, of course, grow up, marry, have children, make a living— realism is satisfied on this score. And yet he never does grow up to be a part of the adult world he observes as a child; the evidence of it is the book itself, in which the mature narrator and the child become one in viewpoint and spirit. David manages what Steerforth and Dora are unable to; he grows up and still remains a child.

The device of looking at the world through the eyes of a child, while it seems to be used consistently to reveal and expose the follies and vices of humanity in a morally neutral light, need not be used with Gosse's wit or Dickens's imaginative success. In fact, the child's perspective, for the very reason that it does reveal, can be used as a coarse obscenity, as it frequently was in Victorian pornography:

> But why do the boys all tease me so,
> And ask if I have a mouse to show?
> They say there's a mouse in Bruce's clothes,
> And when he was cuddling me, it rose![9]

The joke in these unappetizing lines hinges on the child's perception of facts without the ability to comprehend their significance. Of course, the joke only works if the mature reader, who supplies the necessary interpretation, finds child molestation appealing; in other words, to laugh, the reader has to acknowledge the vice the child does not understand and find it attractive. This is something like the mechanism at work in *Father and Son* and *David*

*Copperfield,* where the reader is also presented with the child's unembellished vision of events and asked to supply the ethical distinctions for himself. The pornographic joke, however, differs by eliminating the control imposed by a mature narrator who allows the child to speak through him, as Gosse and Dickens had done: the obscenities of Dickens's Murdstone or Gosse's Plymouth Brethren are considerably blunted by the mature narrator's discretion. In this, the narrator, who allows himself to be the medium through which the child's amoral vision passes, operates like the Freudian ego, softening and refining the willful messages of the id before transmitting them to the strict and aspiring superego; the child's perspective is that of the id; the reader is asked to play the role of superego; and the mature narrator must mollify what might prove to be a vicious correspondence.

But in the pornographic lyric, the guiding hand is withdrawn; we see directly out of the child's eyes, and the vision, unmitigated as it is, either titillates or repels:

> They're not content, though I open wide,
> They grope for something or other inside.

The same choice between titillation and repulsion is frequently present when the child's perspective is used, without the benefit of a guiding narrator, to reveal the behavior of the adult world.

These remarks are meant to preface a discussion of Henry James's *What Maisie Knew* (1897), which, at a considerable pitch of sophistication, employs the same device as the pornographic lyric above. *What Maisie Knew* is James's account of marriage, sex, and society as seen directly through the eyes of a child. To get a feeling for the bluntness of its approach—a bluntness which borders on vulgarity in its overall impact—some allowance must be made for the care and seriousness with which the same topics were handled elsewhere in the period.

*Modern Love,* George Meredith's account of his tortured marriage, was published in 1862; his wife had left him for a painter in 1858, the year following the parliamentary reform of the divorce laws. Husband and wife were made wretched by the experience. The marriage and the poetry stand as a monument to the anxieties and covert barbarisms which afflicted the consciences and domestic lives of the middle class in the era of the Great Exhibition:

> Look, woman, in the West. There wilt thou see
> An amber cradle near the sun's decline:
> Within it, featured even in death divine,
> Is lying a dead infant, slain by thee.    (11)

Whether the echo of Blake is intentional or not, nothing could more fully express the mid-Victorian confusion in the face of unacted desires than these lines: thwarted desire appears in an atomosphere of expiring twilight and innocence betrayed; to nurse an unacted desire brings us to the brink of doom; to act on one pushes us over. No imagery is too grand to present this fearful quandry, and *Modern Love,* closing as it does with a reminiscence of "The Phoenix and the Turtle," spares no grandeur. It is above all else—above its insights, its flashes of jealousy, rage, sorrow, love, and confusion, and above its fine poetry—a poem of utter seriousness, so much so that viewed from the perspective of this century it must be admired as much for the unimpeachable fidelity with

which it clings to the very concepts about which it ex-
presses such confusion as for its psychological and poetic
refinements.

The Divorce Act of 1857, first by bringing the possibility of escape from a bad match within reach of the
middle classes and second by putting a sizable price tag
on the process, undoubtedly went a long way toward
making divorce and its attendant circumstances more
respectable and more businesslike, confining its scandals
and privileges, like those of politics, to the propertied
and monied classes. Yet a couple as unsavory and dis-
affected as Dickens's Lammles, appearing in *Our Mutual
Friend* in 1865, seems to have scrupled to employ the pro-
visions of the Act. Even in their match, which for Dickens
is a perfect ecstasy of thwarted desire, marriage remains a
most solemn and serious affair beyond the scope of mere
law, and its dissolution is presided over by the Furies.

*What Maisie Knew* is the story of not one, but numerous
marriages in ruin and collapse among the London upper
middle class at the end of the century. Maisie, the young
daughter of Ida and Beale Farange, is used as the eyes
of the story; the narrator sees, or pretends to see, no
more than she does as her parents divorce, remarry, separate from their new spouses, and finally leave the young
girl in the charge of her step-parents, who have themselves fallen in love. The story has a symmetry so simple
and so complete that the admiration of it lulls the reader
into a mood of wonder and credulity: Maisie is taken for
a walk in the park by Sir Claude, her mother's second
husband. They discover Ida, who is supposedly in
Belgium, on the arm of another man. The meeting serves
to estrange husband and daughter still further from the

reprobate wife and mother. Not many pages later, Maisie is taken to a circuslike exhibition in Earls Court by her former governess and now stepmother, the present Mrs. Farange, whose attachment to Sir Claude is rapidly developing. The scene in the park is repeated as if in a mirror: the father and husband appears with another woman on his arm. There is a great commotion, with the result that daughter and wife finally have their ties to the father severed.

Of course none of this symmetry would have been possible without the Divorce Act, the revolving door through which Maisie's numerous parents are determined to move simultaneously. But *What Maisie Knew* is uncharacteristic of James's approach to the failure of marriages, which everywhere else preserves, with infinite irony, the fundamental seriousness of Meredith and Dickens. For James, as for Meredith before him, a middle-class marriage is a network of conflicting emotions and tangled desires enacted in the medium of amenities and deserving of the most minute, the most poetic scrutiny. "Ah, what a dusty answer gets the soul / When hot for certainties in this our life!" Meredith had said. The author of *The Portrait of a Lady* and *The Golden Bowl* was not far behind him in searching the bottomless depths of moral ambiguity as seen in the middle-class marriage.

*What Maisie Knew,* however, is a novel of little or no moral ambiguity, at least so far as marriage is concerned. It is rather a book populated by one-dimensional grotesques (James disparaged Dickens for his grotesques, yet here they are in abundance, albeit got up as if for a portrait by Sargent). Maisie's parents are totally discredited from the first page where they are using custody of the child as a weapon against each other. The mother is quickly revealed as a creature of the demimonde, while the father, who spends his nights at the club Chrysanthemum, finally elopes with an obscenely ugly, immensely rich American lady called the Countess, who has a fairly heavy black moustache. The mother is partly, though perhaps not intentionally, redeemed by a penchant for billiards which is matched only by her virtuosity at the game, while Miss Overton, the lovely but scheming governess who marries Maisie's father, has, with Lizzie Eustace, all Becky Sharp's unscrupulous crafts and none of her vitality or charm. Mrs. Wix, Maisie's second governess, develops a passion for Sir Claude, her employer's husband, and this passion she refines first into a duty to "save" him, then into a "moral sense" which finds its fullest expression in the plotted extermination of her rival in love, the former Miss Overton. Only Sir Claude has a trace of moral ambiguity; he seems truly devoted to Maisie's welfare, though otherwise a foppish, spineless creature constantly under the thumb of one Mrs. Farange or another. He too is, in the end, a cad, and gives Maisie over to Mrs. Wix and her "moral sense."

If there is humor in repetition, then there is an abundance of comedy in *What Maisie Knew*. If the characters are, with the sole exception of the quasi narrator, Maisie, awful, they are at least faithful to the symmetry of the book and all awful in the same way. Again and again Maisie meets and welcomes some one of them as her savior from some other one of them, only to discover that they share a common bond—however much they may detest each other—of hypocrisy, deceit, infidelity. In this circus of shabby treatment, Maisie does not even have the means of distinguishing between good and evil; what she knows, or comes to know, is that the adult world around her is an uninterrupted spectacle of folly and betrayal. That she knows good at all can hardly be a function of her environment; she is, as James calls her in his introduction, "a ready vessel for bitterness," a moral *tabula rasa*—a state James here equates with innocence. The solitary ambiguity of the book is that at the end, in offering to give up Mrs. Wix if Sir Claude will give up Mrs. Beale, Maisie makes a proposition that is at once sensibly just and at the same time the first symptom that she has begun to play the same treacherous game as her elders by angling to capture her mother's estranged husband for herself. That Sir Claude would better serve Maisie and himself by accepting is indubitable; that Maisie's motives are untainted is not.

Except in these final pages, however, Maisie remains an innocent: though she observes a host of cruelties, she never passes judgment. "What is immorality?" she inquires of Mrs. Wix in the story's final episode. Maisie's lack of a "moral sense" is as fantastic and as essential to the novel as is its symmetry of structure. Without it, she is no longer the medium through which the world of evil adults around her can work. She must remain "a ready vessel"— and an empty one. In order for the romantic machinations of her elders to succeed, they must use Maisie's innocent moral passivity to their advantage: Miss Overton snares Mr. Farange through her ward; the parents inflict emotional and financial grief on one another by either holding on to her or refusing to accept her; Sir Claude and Mrs. Beale plot their amours around her nursery; even Mrs. Wix's romantic delusions are pinned to her

career as Maisie's guardian. Innocence, then, is a purely
negative state, a void into which all manner of evil in-
intentions will rush. Indeed, it is almost a necessary condition for the propagation of evil; without Maisie's innocent presence, the various cruelties of the novel would not
have been possible. *What Maisie Knew* is a variation on
the Miltonic theme "of knowing good and evil, that is to
say, of knowing good by evil."[10] Maisie's innocence is a
weak, passive thing till she acquires the knowledge to
which the title alludes; what goodness she has is insepar-
able from her growing awareness of the depravity surrounding her.

Maisie's innocence is all the more essential to the style
of narration James has adopted, however. For without
the pretense that the narrator sees only what Maisie does,
and that what Maisie sees, she observes with the lucid
objectivity of an amoral mind, the novel would be completely different. In the hands of an adult, omniscient
narrator, the story of *What Maisie Knew* would be a series
of angry fornications. The same fornications, refracted
through Maisie's young mind, may be presented as insinu-
ations and calculated pieces of reportage, innocent enough
in appearance and only gaining their full value when
interpreted by the mature reader, as in the scene where
Sir Claude meets Mrs. Beale for the first time and discusses his wife's sexual preferences in front of Maisie:

> Sir Claude looked at her hard. "You know who one
> marries, I think. Besides, there are no family-women—
> hanged if there are! None of them want any children—
> hanged if they do!"
> His account of the matter was most interesting, and
> Maisie, as if it were of bad omen for her, stared at

the picture in some dismay. At the same time she felt,
through encircling arms, her protectress hesitate. "You
do come out with things! But you mean her ladyship
doesn't want any—really?"

"Won't hear of them—simply. But she can't help the
one she *has* got."                                    (8)

To an age of cruder contraceptive methods and more
delicate social conventions, such a passage would be titil-
latingly close to obscenity. The narrator, carefully hidden
behind the child, can escape the clear meaning of the
interchange he has created by relating that it "was most
interesting"; could he have escaped as easily in his own
right?

As in *David Copperfield* or *Father and Son,* the adult
world seen through the eyes of James's Maisie is an
absurd parade of human folly and delusion. Unlike them,
however, it is a portrait unrelieved by pathos or hope,
which is almost certainly the result of looking at the world
through the eyes of a child but not allowing the child
to speak through the medium of an older personality, as
the young Gosse and David Copperfield do in their first-
person narratives. The cruelties remain, while the strength
and goodness of the child have no spokesman. In the end,
*What Maisie Knew* shares with pornography the vision of
a guilty but triumphant depravity, which makes it as
unique among James's work as the fact that it is his one
effort at viewing life through the eyes of a child.

# VI

# Children in Children's Literature: James Janeway to Lewis Carroll

The appearance of a children's literature in English is parallel to the emergence of the child figure and shares with it an essential indebtedness to the concept of Original Sin. This chapter briefly examines the use of the child figure in books intended for children, then looks at the emergence of a literature for children based on the child's perspective, and finally applies the results of these inquiries to Lewis Carroll's *Alice in Wonderland*.

No book could better illustrate the connection between the child figure in children's literature and the idea of a fallen universe than James Janeway's *A Token for Children: Being an exact account of the conversion, holy and exemplary lives and joyful deaths of several young children.* Janeway's book, which is perhaps the first book both for and about children (it was published sometime shortly after the Restoration), indicates in text as well as title that the highest reward to which youthful virtue can aspire in this world is to be rid of sinful life entirely. Like the bulk of writers who, in the seventeenth century, began to produce books aimed at children, Janeway was a Dissenter; Bunyan also wrote at least one children's book, *Divine Emblems* (like Janeway's *Token,* there is no certainty as to its date). William Penn is credited with another, *The Spiritual Bee* (1662).

135

But of the Dissenters who were interested in writing books for children, Janeway is among the very few who employ the child figure. And he makes the intention of his portraits of holy youths quite explicit: "Every Mother's Child of you are by Nature Children of Wrath," he admonishes in his introduction, and he goes on to question parents, "Are the Souls of Children of no Value? Are you willing that they should be Brands of Hell? Are you indifferent whether they be damned or saved?"[1] Janeway's is a radical view, not so much for its strict Protestant dogmatism, which, on the question of Original Sin, is firmly rooted in Augustine, but for its insistence that the child is capable of rationally understanding and correcting his fallen condition. Later children's books either assume that the child is incapable of such understanding and hence must be persuaded by appeals to his baser instincts (the morally-instructive story developed from this view), or that the child is both too weak and too irrational to comprehend his sinful condition and hence can only be convinced of the sinful nature of the world around him. From this last view, which is Semipelagian in nature, comes that kind of children's literature which, leaving the child figure to one side, delights in exposing the follies and perversities of adults and life in general; it is neatly exemplified by an early practitioner, Nathaniel Crouch, whose *Winter Evening Entertainments* (early eighteenth century?) is advertised as "milk for children, wisdom for young men, / To teach them that they turn not babes again."[2]

Janeway's strict connection between the child and sin was neither eccentric nor unpopular. *A Token for Children* went through dozens of editions throughout the eighteenth

century and was still in print as late as 1847.[3] His use of
the child figure to instruct children in their fallen nature
became a staple of children's literature. Abraham Chear's
*A Looking-Glass for Children* (c. 1670) illustrates, in one of
its lyrics, the way in which the child figure was employed
to convey the religious dogma throughout the late seventeenth and eighteenth centuries:

> When by spectators I am told
> What beauty doth adorn me,
> Or in a glass when I behold
> How sweetly God did form me,
> Hath God such comeliness bestowed
> And on me made to dwell,
> What pity such a pretty maid
> As I should go to Hell![4]

Isaac Watts's *Divine and Moral Songs for Children* continued this explicit use of the child figure to reinforce
Protestant doctrine, and in the nineteenth century the
tradition was still very much alive in the writings of Mrs.
Sherwood (Mary Martha Butt Sherwood), whose terrifying
accounts of the hell and damnation which attend the evil
actions of childhood are found in her *History of the
Fairchild Family* (1818). In fact, Mrs. Sherwood is, if anything, more direct in her appraisal of the nature of childhood than Janeway had been 150 years earlier; in the
*Fairchild Family,* she states plainly that "All children are
by nature evil, and while they have none but the natural
evil principle to guide them, pious and prudent parents
must check their naughty passions in any way that they
have in their power."[5] Mrs. Sherwood's books sold
throughout the nineteenth century.

Of course, from the Renaissance on, many books were

either written or considered suitable for children which contained none of Janeway's strictures or Mrs. Sherwood's horrors. Curiously, however, these "pleasant" books for children were often satires of adult life which once again tend to confirm that man is involved in some vast and inherent folly. *Robinson Crusoe* and *Gulliver's Travels* were, almost from their publication, considered excellent children's books, as they are today. But where the child figure was employed in children's literature, it remained, to a very late date, tied to the dogma which gives it its impetus as a literary creation.

Even the disciples of Rousseau, when writing in English, seem to fall victim to the general tendency to link childhood and Original Sin. Earlier, in discussing Wordsworth, Thomas Day's *Sandford and Merton* was cited as an example of the way in which an avowed follower of *Emile,* by a number of eccentricities extremely English, produced a work which only marginally reflects its source of inspiration. Maria Edgeworth is another example.[6] Her *The Purple Jar* (1801), also said to be in the tradition of Rousseau, is in fact designed to illuminate the vain willfulness of childhood. In it, the child Rosamond insists upon buying a purple jar of scented water in preference to a solid pair of shoes; the result of this mad assertion of will is that the perfumed water soon becomes a useless bore while the lack of decent footwear leaves Rosamond— or at least her feet—at the mercy of the elements. Here, the *amour de soi* which Rousseau found "good and useful" is vain and foolish, and Nature, far from encouraging it, is ready to punish with rain and cold.

However, while the intention behind the use of the child figure in children's literature remains remarkably constant up to and through the nineteenth century, the tone and style of the child's depiction underwent alteration. The excessive piety and explicit dogmatism of Janeway and Chear gradually gave way to the subtler, more implicitly doctrinaire technique of telling moral stories like Maria Edgeworth's. As mentioned earlier, this was in part due to a belief that children were incapable of the kind of comprehension Janeway and Mrs. Sherwood required of them; but in part this shift of method and tone is the result of an increasing Anglicanization of children's literature. What had begun as the exclusive domain of the Dissenting factions, with whom doctrine was an ever-present concern, became progressively light in style and tone as Anglicans, at once more secure in and less overtly concerned with their dogma, began writing for children. The successful children's writers of the Victorian era who used the child figure in their work were for the most part Church of England; perhaps the two most prominent children's authors, Lewis Carroll and Charles Kingsley, were in orders.

The effect of the Anglican co-option of children's literature, which became virtually total by the end of the last century, is nicely demonstrated by a correspondence in *The Athenaeum* in the 1860s.[7] Remembering a children's lyric from his childhood, the mathematician Augustus De Morgan remarked that it was extremely good poetry except that the "bit of religion thrust in" ruined it:

> For God, who lives above the skies
> Would look with vengeance in His eyes,
> If I should ever dare despise
> My Mother.

The coauthor of the lines, Ann Taylor, who with her brother and sister had, in the first decade of the century, produced several volumes of children's poetry (one had included the lyric "Twinkle, Twinkle, Little Star") was still living, and she agreed that the "bit of religion" no longer seemed appropriate. She accordingly altered the lines to read,

> For could our Father in the skies
> Look down with pleased or loving eyes,
> If ever I could dare despise
> My Mother.

The revision, in which vengeance is implied but not stated, manages to say the same thing as its original, only in a somewhat kinder tone, which is essentially the change which overtook Janeway's conception of children's literature during the nineteenth century.

The presence of the Original Sin dogma behind the child figure in children's literature became increasingly muted during the nineteenth century, and in several children's authors of the Victorian period, it almost disappears. Mrs. Ewing (Juliana Horatia Ewing) is perhaps the best example of this; her stories of middle-class domestic life are peopled by children who are lively, natural, and possessed of a sense of humor. Not that they are without religion. Mrs. Ewing represented the spirit of the Broad Church. The young heroine of her book *A Great Emergency* (1877) ends her narrative with the assurance that she often prays: "I often pray that if ever I am great I may be good too; and sometimes I pray that if I try hard to be good God will let me be great as well,"[8] she says with the proud kind of piety which must have marked the Broad Church in the heyday of the British Empire. Yet even in Mrs. Ewing there are traces of Janeway; her *Story of a Short Life* (1882) portrays the holy and exemplary death of young Leonard, whose dying wish is to hear the hymn, "The Son of God Goes Forth to War," on his deathbed. Similar traces of the strict doctrinaire origin of English children's literature can be found in the two most prolific children's writers of the period, Charlotte Yonge and Mrs. Molesworth (Mary Louisa Molesworth). Charlotte Younge was in her youth a neighbor of John Keble, and her books—there are over 100—are full of the spirit of the Oxford Movement. Mrs. Molesworth's children often find themselves in dark old houses or antique shops, from which they escape into a world of fantasy; her books often confront the child with people and things of great age, as Dickens had, thereby suggesting, however obliquely, the contrast between the Old and New Laws.

Christina Rossetti's poetry for children demonstrates the way in which Victorian authors were able to produce temperate and pleasant works for the young while maintaining a highly orthodox view of the relationship between the child and Original Sin. *Sing-Song* (1872), her volume of lyrics for children, seems to be free of the strictures Janeway and Watts had evoked:

> Angels at the foot
> And angels at the head,
> And like a curly little lamb
> My pretty babe in bed.

But Christina Rossetti's fullest use of the child figure comes in "Goblin Market" (1862), a poem which established its author as one of the chief figures of the Pre-Raphaelite movement. "Goblin Market" does not seem today like a children's poem, yet in its own day it was often included in books for the young.[9] In it, Christina Rossetti's Anglican concept of the fallen nature of man is worked out through the child figure. Behind the poem lies the exceptional devotion to the creed and worship of the Church of England which in her later life monopolized both her poetry and her daily existence. But if "Goblin Market" is orthodox Anglican doctrine, it is also striking poetry, so much so that Swinburne greeted its publication as a lethal blow to the creed of the Philistines and regarded its author as "the Jael who led the host to victory."[10] A closer look at the poem will help to establish the kind of religious view which was considered suitable for children to see and which was at least latently present even in some of the most cheerful works for children written in the Victorian period.

"Goblin Market" is in many respects a version of *Comus* in abbreviated and distorted form: the pentameter is reduced to a purposely halting trimeter, the Lady has shrunk to the size of a child, her tempter is replaced by the goblins, and Sabrina becomes Lizzie, the very proper child whose sacrifice breaks the spell cast over her sister. The poem is Milton as reflected in a fun-house mirror— grotesque, caught somewhere between the sinister and the amusing. In this, at least, it approaches the spirit of Swinburne's own macabre poetry.

More than this, however, "Goblin Market" achieves in its portrait of nature a passion which Swinburne attributed to Byron and Shelley, "a fierce and blind desire which exalts and impels their verse into the high places of emotion and expression. They feed upon nature with a holy hunger, follow her with a divine lust as of gods chasing the daughters of men."[11] The natural world of "Goblin Market" is a sensual banquet, a place where spirits literally chase the daughters of men; but the divinity which presides over the realm of nature where the goblins rule is an evil one. Nature is no longer the "good cateress" of *Comus,* much less Wordsworth's source of transcendent rapture; nature is a raw, sensual power which must either be met on its own terms or must not be met at all.

Where in Wordsworth the essence of childhood is its unity with nature, for Christina Rossetti the child's purity resides in its sheltered retreat from the blandishments of nature's goblins. Laura, the fallen child of the poem, succumbs to the temptations offered "among the brookside rushes":

> You cannot think what figs
> My teeth have met in,
> What melons icy-cold
> Piled on a dish of gold
> Too huge for me to hold,
> What peaches with a velvet nap,
> Pellucid grapes without one seed:
> Odorous indeed must be the mead
> Whereon they grow, and pure the wave they drink.
>
> (173–181)

Laura is not given the Miltonic choice between moderation and indulgence; she must choose between abstinence and excess. The harmless fruits conjured up in the poem's first section invite the child to ruin, and one encounter with them is sufficient to bring Laura "knocking at Death's door" (321).

"Goblin Market" carries this morbid concept of nature through to its logical conclusion in the martyrdom of Lizzie, the redemption of Laura, and their final triumph. After Laura has succumbed to the goblins' invitation to buy their fruits, she is unable to hear their call or find their market again; nature is doubly cruel, not only luring innocence toward ruin, but closing off the avenues by which men might enjoy their depravity once they have fallen. As she grows weaker and weaker, her sister, Lizzie, "weighed no more / Better and worse" (322–323), and determines to buy Laura the fruits she craves. Her sacrifice, however, doesn't have quite the tragic pathos of Adam's for Eve; Lizzie will buy the fruit, but won't eat it herself. "Pluck them and suck them," the goblins cry, and when she will not eat,

> They trod and hustled her,
> Elbowed and jostled her,
> Clawed with their nails,
> Barking, mewing, hissing, mocking,
> Tore her gown and soiled her stockings.
> Twitched her hair out by the roots,
> Stamped upon her tender feet,
> Held her hands and squeezed their fruits
> Against her mouth to make her eat.
>
> (394–407)

The language of the poetry here becomes so graphic that it can no longer be called imagery; it is simple rape. Nature, hiding deceptively behind the seeming beauties which open the poem, is not satisfied until it has violated childhood innocence. But Lizzie escapes intact, and invites her sister to make a Communion feast of her ("Eat me, drink me, love me") for her efforts.

Laura, however, mistakes the meaning of Lizzie's sacrifice:

> "Lizzie, Lizzie, have you tasted
> For my sake the fruit forbidden?"
>
> (478–479)

She does eat and drink Lizzie with kisses of "fear and pain," only to discover that the Eucharist has been a feast of poison. Having passed through these crises, Laura is restored to her former state of purity.

The God who lies behind these images and whose sacrifice is figured in them is hardly the same God who presides over Wordsworth's nature. He is a God who has been put at odds with nature; a God who, when he overcame the world, put the natural world below his feet like a vanquished foe. Insofar as man is a part of nature, he is irreconcilably God's enemy. But man can choose to emulate the state of childhood innocence embodied in Laura and Lizzie, and he does so by avoiding the world of nature entirely. A man's duty to his fellows is

> To lift one if one totters down,
> To strengthen whilst one stands.
>
> (566–567)

If nature, by virtue of man's Fall, has truly become the devil's realm, as Christina Rossetti presents it in "Goblin Market," then perhaps she was right to seek and worship her God from a sickbed in Bloomsbury. Her staunch Anglicanism as expressed in her child figures and children's poems (fiercely in "Goblin Market," gently in *Sing-Song*) illustrates the religious concerns present at least implicitly in the bulk of English children's literature at a time when orthodoxy was being challenged in its letter and its spirit.

While Darwin wrote, while Huxley proclaimed that God had delivered Wilberforce into his hands, while *Essays and Reviews* (1860) questioned even the texts of faith, literature in England, insofar as it employed the child figure, continued to promulgate a nearly orthodox interpretation of the dogma of Original Sin. The generation which came to maturity in the era of the Great War would be inured to attacks on the faith and skeptical of religious tradition. Extreme religious sects such as Gosse's Plymouth Brethren were then a memory, while the Church of England, by the period between the two wars, was known chiefly as the sponsor of the English Folk Dance Society and the institution which, in 1921, tried an archdeacon for adultery in an outmoded ecclesiastical court. Many who took their dogma seriously went to Rome. Yet Englishmen exposed to the literature of the *fin-de-siècle* nursery would have had before them persuasive, if subliminal, arguments in favor of the orthodox doctrine of Original Sin. When he grew up, the same orthodoxy could be found in the child figures of his literature (always excepting Wordsworth). Who can say that this sort of belief and orthodoxy was less real than that of the dwindling number of parishioners in church and chapel?

The children's literature discussed up to this point has shared one common feature; while these poems and books were written for and about children, they were also written as diminutive versions of adult reading. Janeway's *A Token for Children* is a seventeenth-century homily in reduced form; the works of a Mrs. Sherwood or a Mrs.

Ewing mimic the novel or the short story; and as already mentioned, "Goblin Market" is an elfin rendition of *Comus*. The idea of children's literature as a compressed species of adult reading naturally lends itself to Augustine's notion that the child is only a littler replica of his sinful, mature parents. Side by side with the growth of this kind of children's literature, however, another variety of children's books was developing. This variety includes those works not only written for or about children, but from their point of view. Nursery rhymes, fairy tales, and fantasies belong in this group. The distinction between works written for children and those written from the child's perspective is similar to the distinction already observed between first- and third-person narratives of childhood; like *David Copperfield* or *Father and Son,* nursery rhymes and fantasies seem unconcerned with morals and delighted by the absurd.

But what separates *David Copperfield* and *Father and Son* from the nursery rhymes, fairy tales, and fantasies written from the child's point of view is that the former have a mature narrator, either acknowledged or unac-knowledged, whose function it is to render the child's perspective intelligible to adult audiences. In the work of fantasy, however, this mediating adult vanishes and the reader is brought face to face with a world which appears to him illogical, disordered, and unreal. It is the function of children's literature in its purest form to demonstrate (but only to its own satisfaction—anything less would be to compromise its integrity) that precisely the opposite is true; that the fantasy is logical and the reader absurd; that the disorder he had dismissed as childish is a parody of his own world. In *David Copperfield,* after his interview with Mr. Murdstone in the role of his new father, David wanders into the yard and is startled by the appearance in the once-empty dog house of a "great dog—deep-mouthed and black-haired like Him" (3). The true child's perspective has no time or inclination for metaphors. Let Murdstone be a black dog.

Of the types of work written from the child's point of view, nursery rhymes are the most morally neutral. In this, rhymes are exactly the opposite of fables, which are written by adults to point out a moral—usually to other adults. The rhyme which records the history of Solomon Grundy displays the simple and canny observation of facts, devoid of imperatives, which is the trademark of the nursery rhyme form:

> Born on a Monday
> Christened on Tuesday,
> Married on Wednesday,
> Took ill on Thursday,
> Worse on Friday,
> Died on Saturday,
> Buried on Sunday:
> This is the end
> Of Solomon Grundy.[12]

The rhymes cast a very cool eye on life and death; they refuse to be pushed to a position or a conclusion, even in the case of the lady who loved a swine:

> "Wilt thou now have me,
>     Honey," quoth she;
> "Grunt, grunt, grunt," quoth he,
>     And went his way.

This particular rhyme has a wealth of astute observation about the direction of human desires and the ease with which they are frustrated, but it refuses to move beyond observation. Within the world of the rhyme, the pig and the lady live on terms .of absolute equality; whatever is grotesque or perverse in the relationship is imported into the text by the adult reader.

The nursery rhyme can seem either charming or grotesque to adults, or it can be entirely baffling and seem to be both at once:

> Here comes a candle to light you to bed,
> And here comes a chopper to chop off your head.

But in fact the rhymes are meant to be neither charming nor unpleasant; they are not meant to serve any purpose other than strict observation through the eyes of the child mind:

> Around the green gravel the grass grows green,
> And all the pretty maids are plain to be seen;
> Wash them with milk, and clothe them with silk,
> And write their names with a pen and ink.

The final line, typical of nursery rhymes in general, halts what promises to be a soaring flight in mid-course and pulls the idyllic scene back into the realm of the dispassionate, observed fact, which is the milieu of the form.

The basic difference between the nursery rhymes and the instructive form of children's literature inaugurated by Janeway is that the Janeway type is concerned to overcome the vanity of this world while the rhymes are content merely to observe it. The distinction can be seen in a comparison of Christina Rossetti and Edward Lear. The effect of the nursery rhyme may well be the same as that of instructive children's literature, though the method and intent are different. The nonsense verses of Edward Lear, whose career ran more or less parallel to Christina Rossetti's in time, demonstrates how the nursery rhyme form may persuade us of the same facts as instructive children's literature. Lear's verses generally have exactly the same qualities as nursery rhymes: they may seem to adults to be pleasant and charming, or they may, as in the following example, appear morbid and violent:

> Suddenly Mr. Discobbolos
>     Slid from the top of the wall;
>   And beneath it he dug a dreadful trench,
>   And filled it with dynamite, gunpowder gench,
>     And aloud he began to call—
> "Let the wild bee sing,
> And the blue bird hum!
> For the end of your lives has certainly come!"
>     And Mrs. Discobbolos said,
>     "O, W! X! Y! Z!
>     We shall presently all be dead,
> On this ancient runcible wall,
>             Terrible Mr. Discobbolos."[13]

The author of these mad lines is also the author of "The Owl and the Pussy-Cat" which is as appealing as "Mr. and Mrs. Discobbolos" is appalling. By stripping events of logic, viewing them dispassionately, and refusing to pass judgment, Lear's verses, like nursery rhymes, arrive at a self-contained world of nonsense which becomes the basis for a broad view of the world.

This broad view includes a benign fatalism which takes pleasure not in the absurdity it sees in life, but in the fact that absurdity is universal; it revels in having found a unifying principle. If the world is absurd, at least it is perfectly absurd, and both Lear and nursery rhymes make their poetry reflect this peculiar perfection.

Fairy tales also portray an absurd world, but what distinguishes them from nursery rhymes is a high sense of justice. Unlike the nursery rhyme, the fairy tale has a strong inclination built into it to deal with questions of "right" and "wrong"; it is, on the whole, a much more "grown-up" literature. Fairy tales have a plot, which naturally gives them not only a sense of mature logic, but lends them to moral interpretation as well, since any series of events leading to a logical conclusion carries an implicit or explicit message, no matter how ambiguous. The fairy tale's plot may very well stem from its heightened sense of injury done to the child figure or child surrogate. "In the little world in which children have their existence whosoever brings them up, there is nothing so finely perceived and so finely felt, as injustice," says Pip in *Great Expectations,* and the statement may serve as an introduction to fairy tales, in which the child figure or substitute is usually the passive victim of some adult injustice. Out of this sense of injustice comes the child's first participation with the system of adult values.

The two strains of children's literature—that in which the child is instructed about the folly of the world and that in which the child mind merely observes these follies— are brought together in Lewis Carroll's *Alice in Wonderland* (1865). In fact, Lewis Carroll represents the highpoint of both traditions. There is plenty of the nursery rhyme's absurdity in *Alice:* perhaps the best example of it is Alice's translation of Isaac Watts's "How doth the little busy bee" into "How doth the little crocodile." Carroll delighted in parodies of children's authors who had written in the cautionary vein. His parodies, like Lear's nonsense, are so close to the spirit of the nursery rhyme that by their presence alone *Alice* seems to belong to the class of children's literature which is content to observe rather than moralize.

But Carroll also belongs to the group of Anglican children's writers who continued to purvey Janeway's Protestant conception of Original Sin, while modifying his tone and technique. As Charles Lutwidge Dodgson, Carroll was a deacon of the Church of England. He was so careful of his piety that in writing *Through the Looking-Glass* (1871) he changed the passion flower in "The Garden of Live Flowers" to a tiger-lily on learning that the passion flower referred to the Crucifixion.[14] His children's books are orthodox as well as absurd. From the conclusion of *Alice,* it is clear Carroll meant his readers to derive a benefit from the book which would inform their future years; when Alice has awoken and told her sister about Wonderland, the sister

> pictured to herself how this same little sister of hers would, in the after-time, be herself a grown woman; and how she would keep, through all her riper years, the simple and loving heart of her childhood; and how she would gather about her other little children, and make their eyes bright and eager with many a strange tale, perhaps even with the dream of Wonderland of long ago; and how she would feel with all their simple sorrows, and find pleasure in all their simple joys, remembering her own child-life, and the happy summer days.

This is the end of the book, and it is remarkably similar to the final lines of "Goblin Market," which preceded it by four years. Christina Rossetti pictures Lizzie and Laura as grown-ups with children of their own:

> Laura would call the little ones
> And tell them of her early prime,
> Those pleasant days long gone
> Of not-returning time;
> Would talk about the haunted glen,
> The wicked quaint fruit-merchant men,
> Their fruits like honey to the throat
> But poison to the blood.    (548–555)

Nor are *Alice* and "Goblin Market" alike only in their conclusions. Much of Christina Rossetti's orthodoxy can be found in the structure of *Alice*.

The first hint that *Alice* is indeed working with the same Christian concepts which surround the child figure elsewhere in English literature comes in chapter one: "Down, down, down. Would the fall *never* come to an end? 'I wonder how many miles I've fallen by this time?' she said aloud." The Wonderland into which Alice falls is in many respects like the elfin nature which seduces Laura in "Goblin Market." In "Goblin Market," however, it is Laura who finds the goblins' world seductive while the reader sees the evil behind it; in Alice the situation is reversed: Alice consistently finds Wonderland curious, foolish, and finally "stuff and nonsense" (12), while the reader is seduced by its attractions.

These attractions, which are presented in the absurd view of the nursery rhyme, are the allures of a fallen universe. Wonderland is a realm of Original Sin where, quite literally, everyone lies under sentence of death. This is the realm the nursery rhyme uncritically observes. Here, however, the nursery rhyme's observation has been set in a framework designed to involve the reader's critical faculties. The book is structured to have epic pretensions. Like *Through the Looking-Glass,* it has twelve books, the required Vergilian number; Alice's fall down the hole is a descent into the underworld as well as a reminder of the Original Sin theme; and Alice herself is reminiscent of Aeneas in her statuesque, Tory respectability, which is at once aloof from, and necessary to, the action of the book. The imaginative quality of *Alice* is that of the nursery rhyme, but its form is that of a mock epic and its purpose is a judgment of the fallen world through its central character, Alice. Dickens had adapted the epic and the child figure to this same end in *Dombey and Son*.

As in *Through the Looking-Glass,* the world Alice enters in *Alice in Wonderland* has reversed the true and proper meanings of things, though in Wonderland this reversal of meanings has a more obviously moral significance than in the *Looking-Glass* world. Chapter I offers a tantalizing vision of what appears to be a veritable Eden, "the loveliest garden you ever saw." But Alice's attempts to enter the garden are thwarted, in a parody of the Communion service, by Alice's consumption of the mysterious offerings which come complete with the mock-priestly instructions, "DRINK ME" and "EAT ME." While not quite a black mass, Alice's meal does have exactly the opposite effect of the true Communion; far from opening Eden to her, it makes her far too large to enter. As a result, there follows the deluge of tears, which amounts to Noah's flood, "crowded with the birds and animals that had fallen into it" (2).

Next follow scenes of ever-escalating venalities: the mouse's churlishness; the White Rabbit's fastidious vexation, which threatens Alice with the loss of an arm; the caterpillar's contemptuous indifference; the savagery of the Duchess, matched only by her ugliness; the rudeness of the tea party, which almost engulfs Alice in an eternity of mad repetition reminiscent of Sisyphus's punishment. Finally, Alice enters the garden she had seen through the small door. But the supposed Eden is no paradise at all; the first thing she sees on entering it is a rosetree, which the gardeners are painting red. The idea recalls Spenser's Bower of Bliss, "That nature's work by art can imitate." The Queen's croquet ground is a place where everyone has been sentenced to death, and the story ends at precisely the moment Alice is included in this "everyone":

> "Hold your tongue!" said the Queen, turning purple.
> "I won't!" said Alice.
> "Off with her head!" the Queen shouted at the top of her voice. Nobody moved.
> "Who cares for *you*?" said Alice (she had grown to her full size by this time). "You're nothing but a pack of cards!"
> At this the whole pack rose up into the air, and came flying down upon her; she gave a little scream, half of fright and half of anger, and tried to beat them off, and found herself lying on the bank, with her head in the lap of her sister, who was gently brushing away some dead leaves. (12)

In the end, the Wonderland creatures turn out to be "some dead leaves," an image which invites us to recall Milton's own underworld creatures,

> who lay intrans't
> Thick as Autumnal Leaves that strow the Brooks
> In Vallombrosa. (1.301–303)

If *Alice in Wonderland,* like a nursery rhyme, looks at the adult world with the eyes of childhood, it also takes that vision and by framing it in a mock-epic format roundly condemns what it sees. Wonderland is the world after the

Fall. The paradise behind the door is a mirror image of what it seems, a place of death where living creatures are perverted from their natural functions to suit the Queen's purposes—flamingoes as mallets, hedgehogs as balls, men as wickets. The story concludes with the monumental injustice of the trial, at which Alice realizes that to escape from the sentence of death the Queen imposes, she has but to assert her contempt for the entire proceedings.

The gradually increasing threats of Wonderland are parallelled and in a sense presented by the steady corruption of language from chapter to chapter, a process which puzzles and then infuriates Alice. Carroll himself seems to have equated the misuse of language with the perversion of the world at large, and as in the following introduction to his *Symbolic Logic* (1897), a book somewhat whimsically intended for children, regarded the correct use of words as a complete defense against worldly error:

> Once master the machinery of Symbolic Logic, and you have a mental occupation always at hand, . . . and one that will be of real *use* to you in *any* subject you may take up. It will give you clearness of thought—the ability to *see your way* through a puzzle—the habit of arranging your ideas in an orderly and get-at-able form—and more valuable than all, the power to detect *fallacies,* and to tear to pieces the flimsy illogical arguments, which you will so continuously encounter in books, in newspapers, in speeches, and even in sermons, and which so easily delude those who have never taken the trouble to master this fascinating Art.[15]

In Wonderland, the abuse of language begins with the simple lack of information in the directions "EAT ME" and "DRINK ME" and ends with the verbal mockery of justice

which is the Knave's trial. In between lie various failures
to impart information correctly, such as the caterpillar's,
which almost results in Alice's disintegration; false syllogisms; and that lowest form of wit, the pun. Part of what
makes *Alice in Wonderland* palatable, where other children's books employing the same devices are preciously
trite, is the vigor with which these abuses are persecuted
even as they are employed; the heroine stands resolutely
above them, so that we see the corruption of language as
the tool which has built the false Eden.

The underground world, as a reflection of life, seems to
hold little promise of a happy destiny for Alice; in fact,
her destiny depends on her "ability to see her way through
a puzzle" and "tear to pieces the flimsy illogical arguments," which she continuously encounters. Aeneas had
his golden bough to bring him back alive from the land
of the dead; Alice likewise has a magical charm, preserving
her for a glorious destiny, in her perception of events in
terms of symbolic logic. She stoutly refuses to call the
events she sees in Wonderland wrong—ethical distinctions
are part of the structure of the underworld itself, culminating in the Knave's trial; instead, she prefers to see
things as either sensible or stupid. She is allowed her
share of mistakes, like any epic hero, but as the story
moves along, her ability to see things in the proper absurdist perspective improves rapidly. She has an instinctive
contempt for the humdrum moralizing of Isaac Watts's
"How doth the little busy bee," and transforms it from
religious propaganda into a nursery rhyme. The same process is repeated with Southey's didactic piece, which
becomes "You are Old, Father William." These reductions
to absurdity are her own invention, and not a part of

Wonderland itself. The Caterpillar chastises her for not getting "Father William" "right," and the Mad Hatter stands under sentence of death for his own absurdist effort with "Twinkle, Twinkle, Little Bat."

Along with the preference for a sense-nonsense distinction over a moral system comes the detached acceptance of things as they are that marks the nursery rhyme view of events. When the Duchess's baby turns into a pig, "she felt that it would be quite absurd for her to carry it any further. So she set the little creature down and felt quite relieved to see it trot away quietly into the wood. 'If it had grown up,' she said to herself, 'it would have made a dreadfully ugly child: but it makes rather a handsome pig, I think'" (6). In this genial acceptance of the bizarre, there is an almost mystical belief in the ability of life, even in its most perverse and grotesque manifestations, to come around at last to fitting conclusions. These conclusions may disturb or repel us, but to the child, they seem just and fair. The Wonderland population has no notion of this natural fitness. The Duchess is forever looking for the moral of things, the Hatter has literally killed time, and the Queen who reigns over them all gets the purpose of everything backward, from the role of king and queen, which she has reversed, to the natural order of justice: "'No, no!' said the Queen. 'Sentence first—verdict afterwards.' 'Stuff and nonsense!' said Alice loudly" (12). Alice overturns the false order of Wonderland with the faith and assurance of the symbolic logician destroying a fallacious syllogism, and in a sense she sees the world around her as the work of a logician God. Its terms and propositions need not be "right" in the way the Queen or the Duchess would have them; they must merely conform to

an inner truth, as in one of Carroll's own syllogisms
(which is strictly logical):

> A prudent man shuns hyaenas;
> No banker is imprudent.
> No banker fails to shun hyaenas.[16]

A cosmos constructed along these same lines does not
lend itself to interpretation or understanding by the logic
or morality of Wonderland; it must be accepted with implicit faith in the truthfulness of the great Logician to his
own premises. Possessing this faith, Alice passes through
Wonderland victoriously, as if with Aeneas's golden bough.
Carroll is, like Aquinas and Dante before him, a Semipelagian; he cannot tolerate the idea of children as part
of the world of sin, and in *Alice in Wonderland,* the
heroine stands resolutely apart from the machinery of
Original Sin. Yet how much hope is there in this Semipelagian view, and what threat does it represent to
Augustine's dogma? Alice herself may be outside the pale
of Original Sin, but the value of her observations and
adventures in Wonderland is minimal for the adult world.
Her dream of Wonderland is real enough to her child's
mind, but its point is lost on the adult world to which it
is presented. Like Aeneas's memory of the underworld,
Alice's dream is destined to seem unreal to us—enter-
tainingly absurd—even though it contains essential truths,
because we are the descendants of Adam. Alice's dream
has passed through the Gate of Ivory which is the fallen
imagination of man:

> altera candenti perfecta nitens elephanto,
> sed falsa ad caelum mittunt insomnia manes.

# Notes

## Chapter I

1. *Iliad* 6.466–502.
2. *Ethics* 1111b; ed. Richard McKeon, *The Basic Works of Aristotle* (New York: Random House, 1941), pp. 967–968.
3. *Ethics* 1100a; p. 946.
4. *Aeneid* 2.679–704.
5. *"Vascula oris angusti," De institutione oratoria* 1.2.28. Translations in the text which are not otherwise acknowledged are by the author.
6. *Laws* 808D; trans. Benjamin Jowett, *The Dialogues of Plato,* 2 vols. (1871; reprint ed., Oxford: Oxford University Press, 1964), 2:245.
7. 44B–C; trans. Francis M. Cornford, *Plato's Cosmology* (1937; reprint ed., New York: Bobbs-Merrill, n.d.), p. 150.
8. E. R. Dodds, "From Shame-Culture to Guilt-Culture," *The Greeks and the Irrational* (1951; reprint ed., Berkeley: University of California Press, 1971), pp. 28–63.
9. *"Consolatio ad uxorem," Moralia,* 612A–B; trans. Rex Warner, *Moral Essays* (Harmondsworth: Penguin, 1971), p. 185.
10. See J. B. Leishman, *The Art of Marvell's Poetry* (New York: Funk and Wagnalls, 1966), pp. 165–189, which gives a concise history of "young love" poetry, tracing it back to Horace and two minor poems in the Greek Anthology (5.111 and 5.124).
11. This brief summary of Pelagius's life is based on John Ferguson, *Pelagius* (London: W. Heffer, 1956).
12. *De natura et gratia* 236.
13. *Phaedrus* 248C.
14. *Phaedrus* 247C.
15. *Adversus haereses* 5.16.3. This discussion of the development of the doctrine of Original Sin owes a great deal to

N. P. Williams's *The Ideas of the Fall and of Original Sin* (London: Longmans, Green, 1927), which places, as I do, strong emphasis upon Augustine's special role in the formulation of this dogma. For the opposing view that the concept of Original Sin was in fact well established in the early Church, see Frederick R. Tennant, *The Sources of the Doctrines of the Fall and Original Sin* (1903; reprint ed., New York: Schocken Books, 1968). I believe a reading of the original sources and of Adolf Harnack's still authoritative *History of Dogma*, trans. Neil Buchanan, 7 vols. (1900; reprint ed., New York: Dover, 1961), confirms the view that Augustine, under the influence of his teacher, Ambrose, must be regarded as virtually the single-handed champion of the doctrine of Original Sin.

16. Irenaeus compares baptism to Christ's anointing the eyes of the blind man in John 9:6–7. The operation of the sacrament is not to remove an original stain, but to enable the baptized person "cognosceret Plasmatorem et disceret Dominum eum qui donavit ei vitam," "to understand his Maker and know the Master who has given him life." *Adversus haereses* 5.15.3. This conception of baptism is far and away more positive than Augustine's.

17. In *De principiis* 2.9, Origen says of man that "the causes of his diversity are in himself and antecedent to his bodily birth." For a full discussion of Origen's conception of the Fall, which is greatly indebted to the *Phaedrus,* see Harnack, *History of Dogma,* 2:361–365.

18. *De baptismo* 18.

19. Henry Bettenson, ed., *Documents of the Christian Church* (London: Oxford University Press, 1963), p. 75.

20. See Gregory of Nyssa's baptismal sermon in *Baptism,* ed. Andre Hamman (New York: Alba House, 1967), pp. 123–137.

21. Second canon of the Council of Carthage, 417, in Bettenson, *Documents of the Christian Church,* p. 59.

22. Augustine *Confessions* 1.7; trans. E. B. Pusey (1838; New York: E. P. Dutton, 1951), p. 7.

23. Williams, *Original Sin*, p. 376.

24. Ibid., p. 391.

25. Ibid., pp. 419–421.

26. For a history of the role of the child in the social life of Europe before the nineteenth century, the classic study is Philippe Ariès, *L'Enfant et la vie sous l'ancien régime,* translated as *Centuries of Childhood* by Robert Baldick (New York: Alfred Knopf, 1962).

## Chapter II

1. E. V. Gordon, ed., *Pearl* (Oxford: Clarendon Press, 1953), ll. 483–486.

2. See the discussion of baptism, ll. 625–660.

3. *An Essay Concerning Human Understanding,* 2 vols. (Oxford: Clarendon Press, 1894), 1:250.

4. Ibid., 1:67.

5. Ibid., 1:230.

6. Cited in *The Complete Poems of Thomas Gray,* ed. H. W. Starr and J. R. Hendrickson (Oxford: Clarendon Press, 1966), pp. 203–204.

7. Ibid., p. 203.

8. In Wilbur L. Cross, *The Life and Times of Laurence Sterne,* 3rd ed. (New Haven: Yale University Press, 1929), p. 269.

9. For a brief discussion of the difficulties surrounding Sterne's citation of the Carthaginian canons, see *Tristram Shandy,* ed. James Aiken Work (New York: Odyssey Press, 1940), p. 340n.

10. *The Sermons of Mr. Yorick,* 2 vols. (New York: Clonmel Society, 1904), 1:172–173.

11. See Martin C. Battestin, *The Moral Basis of Fielding's Art: A Study of Joseph Andrews* (Middletown, Conn.: Wesleyan University Press, 1959), p. 152.

12. "An Essay on the Knowledge of the Characters of Men," *The Complete Works of Henry Fielding,* 18 vols. (London: Frank Cass, 1967), 14:281–282.

## Chapter III

1. See A. Charles Babenroth, *English Childhood: Words-worth's Treatment of Childhood in Light of English Poetry from Prior to Crabbe,* Columbia University Studies in English and Comparative Literature, vol. 70 (New York: Columbia University Press, 1922); Babenroth's title is itself a description of the alterations at work in the child figure during the eighteenth century.

2. Jean Jacques Rousseau, *Emile, Julie and Other Writings,* trans. R. L. Archer (Woodbury, N.Y.: Barron's Educational Series, 1964), p. 95.

3. *Of Education,* in *Complete Poems and Major Prose* (New York: Odyssey Press, 1957), p. 631.

4. *Emile, Julie and Other Writings,* pp. 97–98.

5. Ibid., p. 29.

6. *De gestis pelagii* 23; in Bettenson, *Documents of the Christian Church,* pp. 53–54.

7. *Emile, Julie and Other Writings,* p. 64.

8. *Emile,* trans. William Boyd (New York: Teachers College Press, 1960), p. 65.

9. "Against Scoffing and Calling Names," *Songs, Divine and Moral* (1720), in *The Poems of Watts,* 2 vols. (Chiswick, 1822), 2:124.

10. In Michael Sadler, *Thomas Day: An English Disciple of Rousseau* (Cambridge: Cambridge University Press, 1928), p. 8.

11. "Evening Walk," l. 21.

12. "To H.C.: Six Years Old" (composed 1802), ll. 11–14, 27–29.

13. Ben Jonson uses the idea in "Epitaph on S.P. a Child of Q. El. Chappel" (1615): "But, being so much too good for earth, / Heaven vowes to keepe him." Milton's "Fair Infant Dying of a Cough" (1628) is sent to earth "to set the hearts of men on fire / To scorn the sordid world, and unto Heav'n aspire" (62–63).

14. For the connection between the child and the noble savage, see Hoxie Neale Fairchild, "The Child of Nature and

the Noble Savage," *The Noble Savage: A Study in Romantic Naturalism,* Columbia University Studies in English and Comparative Literature, vol. 90 (New York: Columbia University Press, 1928), pp. 365–385.

15. Peter Coveney says of Wordsworth's "conversion" that he "confronted the moral problems of the early Victorian period with an Anglican orthodoxy. As Professor Willey has said of him: 'there is a steady retreat towards the religious sources of his mysticism, and grace supplants the visionary gleam'"; *The Image of Childhood* (Harmondsworth: Penguin Books, 1967), p. 81.

16. In George McLean Harper, *William Wordsworth: His Life, Works, and Influence,* 2 vols. (New York: Russell and Russell, 1960), 2:557.

17. In Alexander Gilchrist, *The Life of William Blake* (New York: Dodd, Mead, 1906), p. 2.

18. Critics admit Blake's orthodoxy on the Fall, although they often attempt to compound it with some doctrinal impurity: Northrop Frye says Blake was part Gnostic: *Fearful Symmetry: A Study of William Blake* (1947; reprint ed., Boston: Beacon Press, 1962), p. 41. George Mills Harper says Blake's idea of the Fall was conditioned by the Dionysiac mysteries and Neoplatonism: "The Fall of Man," *The Neoplatonism of William Blake* (Chapel Hill: University of North Carolina Press, 1961), pp. 228–245. Perhaps the measure of Blake's orthodoxy should be the scene (Gilchrist, *Blake,* p. 115) of Blake and his wife reading *Paradise Lost* in their garden, stripped to the nude. Much of Blake's scorn was reserved for those who did not share an equally literal reading of Christian myth. He took his Fall strictly and seriously.

19. Dorothy Marshall, *The English Poor in the Eighteenth Century* (London: George Routledge and Sons, 1926), p. 98; Jonas Hanway, *Letters to the Guardians of the Infant Poor* (London, 1767), pp. 74ff.

20. Edwin Hodder, *The Life and Work of the Seventh Earl of Shaftesbury,* 3 vols. (London, 1888), 3:520.

21. Ibid., 3:519.

22. Ibid., 1:441–442.

23. Ibid., 1:503.

24. Ibid., 2:143.

25. Hanway, *A Sentimental History of Chimney-Sweepers in London and Westminster* (London, 1785); James Montgomery, ed., *The Chimney-Sweeper's Friend and Climbing-Boy's Album* (London, 1824). Note how Hanway makes the connection between childhood and sentiment.

26. *London Labour and the London Poor,* 4 vols. (1861–1862; reprint ed., New York: Dover, 1968), 2:338–378.

## Chapter IV

1. Una Pope-Hennessy, *Charles Dickens* (New York: Howell, Soskin, 1946), pp. 150–151.

2. Stephen Marcus, *Dickens: From Pickwick to Dombey* (New York: Basic Books, 1965), p. 129.

3. "Preface," *The Old Curiosity Shop* (London: Oxford University Press, 1951), p. xi.

4. John Forster, *The Life of Charles Dickens,* 2 vols. (1872–1874; reprint ed., London: J. M. Dent, 1966), 1:120.

5. Ibid., 1:123.

6. "Chaucer's Pardoner, The Scriptural Eunuch, and *The Pardoner's Tale,*" *Speculum,* 30 (1955), reprinted in Richard Schoeck and Jerome Taylor, eds. *Chaucer Criticism,* 2 vols. (Notre Dame Books, 1960), 1:221–244.

7. Forster, *Dickens,* 2:422; the expression comes from Dickens's will, which urged his children to "try to guide themselves by the teaching of the New Testament in its broad spirit, and to put no faith in any man's narrow construction of its letter here or there."

8. *"Our Mutual Friend,"* *The Nation,* 1 (1865), reprinted in *Selected Literary Criticism of Henry James,* ed. Morris Shapiro (New York: McGraw-Hill, 1965), p. 7.

9. See Gerald Willen, ed., *A Casebook on Henry James's*

*The Turn of the Screw* (New York: Thomas Y. Crowell, 1960) for a compendium of this criticism.

10. In Charles F. Harrold and William D. Templeman, eds., *English Prose of the Victorian Era* (New York: Oxford University Press, 1938), p. 1477.

11. In J. W. Cross, *George Eliot's Life,* 2 vols. (New York, 1885), 2:210.

12. Ibid., 2:220.

13. *A System of Logic* (1843; reprint ed., London: Longmans, 1961), p. 565.

14. *Biographia Literaria* (New York, 1884), pp. 481–482.

15. *Autobiography* (1873; reprint ed., New York: Columbia University Press, 1944), p. 103.

16. Ibid., p. 104.

17. "Nature" (1874), in Harrold and Templeman, *English Prose of the Victorian Era,* p. 734.

18. Ibid., p. 747.

19. Darwin's essay, written in 1840, appeared in· *Mind,* 2, no. 7 (July, 1877), 292ff; Lewes's article appeared in the same publication, 2, no. 6 (April, 1877), 160ff.

20. *The British Critic and Quarterly Theological Review,* 24 (October, 1843), 356, 417.

21. *Interpretations of Poetry and Religion* (1900; reprint ed., New York: Harper and Brothers, 1957), p. 77.

## Chapter V

1. Wayne Shumaker, *English Autobiography,* University of California English Studies, no. 8 (Berkeley: University of California Press, 1954), p. 5.

2. *A History of Autobiography in Antiquity,* trans. E. W. Dickes, 2 vols. (London: Routledge and Kegan Paul, 1950), 1:4.

3. Shumaker, *English Autobiography,* pp. 22–23.

4. *The Life and Work of Sigmund Freud* (New York: Anchor Books, 1963), p. 237.

5. *The Naturalist of the Sea-Shore* (London: William Heinemann, 1896), p. 351.

6. Forster, *Dickens,* 2:107.

7. "The Two Scrooges," *The Wound and the Bow* (1941; reprinted, Oxford University Press, 1947), p. 43.

8. Angus Wilson, *The World of Charles Dickens* (New York: Viking, 1970), p. 216.

9. "Missy's Thoughts," *The Pearl,* 6 (December, 1879), reprinted in *The Pearl* (New York: Grove Press, 1968), pp. 196–197.

10. *Areopagitica,* in *Complete Poetry and Major Prose,* p. 728.


## Chapter VI

1. *A Token for Children* (Boston, 1771), p. 4.

2. Cited in F. J. Harvey Darton, *Children's Books in England* (Cambridge: Cambridge University Press, 1932), p. 62.

3. Ibid., p. 56.

4. Cited in Emelyn E. Gardner and Eloise Ramsey, *A Handbook of Children's Literature* (New York: Scott, Foresman, 1927) but incorrectly attributed to Janeway; see Darton, *Children's Books in England,* p. 61.

5. *History of the Fairchild Family* (London, n.d.), p. 13.

6. Darton links her with Day in his chapter nine, pp. 141–157 on the "French Influence": "Maria Edgeworth, on the other hand, had the essential humanity which Rousseau at his best inspired," *Children's Books in England,* p. 144.

7. The story of this correspondence is given in Darton, *Children's Books in England,* pp. 189–190.

8. *A Great Emergency* (reprint ed., New York: Schocken Books, 1969), pp. 112–113.

9. Darton discusses the acceptance of "Goblin Market" as children's verse, *Children's Books in England,* p. 282; in this country, J. B. Lippincott published a children's edition of the poem as late as 1941.

10. Edmund Gosse and T. J. Wise, eds., *The Complete Works*

*of Algernon Charles Swinburne,* 20 vols. (London: William Heinemann, 1927), vol. 19, *The Life of Algernon Charles Swinburne* by Edmund Gosse, p. 127.

11. "Byron" (1866), in *Swinburne: Selected Poetry and Prose,* ed. John D. Rosenberg (New York: Random House, 1968), p. 347.

12. The first known edition of nursery rhymes in English is *Tommy Thumb's Pretty Song Book* (1744), of which one copy survives, in the British Museum; *Mother Goose's Melody* appeared in London, 1791. The original Mother Goose, Charles Perrault's *Contes de ma mere l'oie,* was published in Paris, 1698; it contains not rhymes, but fairy tales with morals appended. The collection of nursery rhymes used here is Andrew Lang's *The Nursery Rhyme Book* (1897; reprint ed., New York: Dover Books, 1972).

13. "Mr. and Mrs. Discobbolos," Second Part (1877), *The Complete Nonsense of Edward Lear* (New York: Dover Books, 1951), p. 250.

14. *The Annotated Alice,* ed. Martin Gardner (New York: World Publishing, 1963), p. 200.

15. "Introduction," *Symbolic Logic* (New York: Dover Books, 1958), p. xvii.

16. Ibid., pp. 109, 152.

# Bibliography

Ariès, Philippe. *Centuries of Childhood (L'enfant et la vie sous l'ancien régime)*. Trans. Robert Baldick. New York: Alfred Knopf, 1962.

Aristotle. *Nicomachean Ethics,* in *The Basic Works of Aristotle.* Ed. Richard McKeon. New York: Random House, 1941.

Auerbach, Nina. "Alice in Wonderland: A Curious Child." *Victorian Studies,* 17 (September 1973), 31–48.

Augustine. *Confessions.* Trans. E. B. Pusey. 1838; rpt. New York: E. P. Dutton, 1951.

————. *La Crise Pélagienne.* Vol. 21 of *Oeuvres, Troisième Serie: La Grâce.* Eds. G. de Plinval and J. de la Tullaye. Bruges: Desclée de Brouwer, 1966.

Ault, Norman, ed. *Elizabethan Lyrics.* 4th ed.; London: Longmans, 1966.

Babenroth, A. Charles. *English Childhood: Wordsworth's Treatment of Childhood in the Light of English Poetry from Prior to Crabbe.* Vol. 70 of Columbia University Studies in English and Comparative Literature. New York: Columbia University Press, 1922.

Barth, J. Robert. *Coleridge and Christian Doctrine.* Cambridge: Harvard University Press, 1969.

Battenhouse, Roy W., ed. *A Companion to the Study of St. Augustine.* New York: Oxford University Press, 1955.

Battestin, Martin C. *The Moral Basis of Fielding's Art: A Study of Joseph Andrews.* Middletown, Conn.: Wesleyan University Press, 1959.

Beach, Joseph Warren. *The Concept of Nature in Nineteenth Century English Poetry.* New York: Macmillan, 1936.

Bettenson, Henry, ed. *Documents of the Christian Church.* London: Oxford University Press, 1963.

Bewley, Marius. "Appearance and Reality in Henry James." *Scrutiny,* 17 (Summer 1950), 90–114.

Birch, A. H. "A Fifth Century Apostle of Free Will." *Hibbert Journal,* 46 (October 1947), 56–62. On Pelagius.

Blake, William. *The Complete Writings.* Ed. Geoffrey Keynes. New York: Random House, 1957.

Bready, J. Wesley. *Lord Shaftesbury and Social-Industrial Progress.* London: George Allen and Unwin, 1926.

*British Critic and Quarterly Theological Review.* Unsigned review of John Stuart Mill's *A System of Logic.* Vol. 34 (October 1843), 349–427.

Brown, Carleton F. "The Author of *The Pearl* Considered in the Light of His Theological Opinions." *PMLA,* N.S. 12 (1904), 115–152.

Carcopino, Jérôme. *Daily Life in Ancient Rome.* New Haven: Yale University Press, 1940.

Carroll, David R. "*Silas Marner:* Reversing the Oracles of Religion," in *Literary Monographs,* 1. Madison: University of Wisconsin Press, 1967. 167–200.

Carroll, Lewis. *The Annotated Alice: Alice's Adventures in Wonderland and Through the Looking-Glass.* Ed. Martin Gardner. New York: World, 1963.

———. *Symbolic Logic.* 1897; rpt. New York: Dover Books, 1958.

Charteris, Evan. *The Life and Letters of Sir Edmund Gosse.* London: Heinemann, 1931.

Coleridge, Samuel Taylor. *Biographia Literaria; or, Biographical Sketches of My Life and Opinions.* New York: Harper and Brothers, 1853.

Collingwood, Stuart Dodgson. *The Life and Letters of Lewis Carroll.* London: T. Fisher Unwin, 1898.

Collins, Philip. *Dickens and Education.* London: Macmillan, 1963.

Commager, Steele. *The Odes of Horace.* New Haven: Yale University Press, 1962.

Coveney, Peter. *The Image of Childhood: The Individual and Society: A Study of the Theme in English Literature.* Harmondsworth: Penguin Books, 1967.

Cross, J. W. *George Eliot's Life as Related in Her Letters and Journals.* 3 vols. New York: Harper and Brothers, 1885.

Cross, Wilbur L. *The Life and Times of Laurence Sterne.* 3rd ed. New Haven, Yale University Press, 1929.

Daiches, David. "The Sexless Sentimentalist." *The Listener,* 63 (May 1960), 841–843. On J. M. Barrie.

Darton, F. J. Harvey. *Children's Books in England: Five Centuries of Social Life.* Cambridge: Cambridge University Press, 1932.

Darwin, Charles. "A Biographical Sketch of an Infant." *Mind,* 3 (July 1877), 285–294.

Davies, Horton. *Worship and Theology in England.* 5 vols. Princeton: Princeton University Press, 1961–.

Day, Thomas. *The History of Sandford and Merton.* New York: Harper, 1856.

Dickens, Charles. *Bleak House.* New York: Oxford University Press, 1948.

———. *David Copperfield.* New York: Oxford University Press, 1926.

———. *Dombey and Son.* New York: Oxford University Press, 1968.

———. *The Old Curiosity Shop.* New York: Oxford University Press, 1951.

———. *Our Mutual Friend.* New York: Oxford University Press, 1959.

Dodds, E. R. *The Greeks and the Irrational.* 1951; rpt. Berkeley: University of California Press, 1971.

Doherty, Paul C. "Hopkins' 'Spring and Fall: To a Young Child.'" *Victorian Poetry,* 5 (Summer 1967), 140–143.

Donovan, Frank. *Dickens and Youth.* New York: Dodd, Mead, 1968.

Edel, Leon. *Henry James.* 5 vols. Philadelphia: J. B. Lippincott, 1953–1972.

Edgeworth, Maria. *The Purple Jar and Other Tales.* London: Routledge, Warne and Routledge, 1862.

Eliot, George. *The Mill on the Floss.* London: J. M. Dent, 1952.

———. *Silas Marner: The Weaver of Raveloe.* London: Oxford University Press, 1913.

Ellis, Alec. *A History of Children's Reading and Literature.* London: Pergamon Press, 1968.

Empson, William. *Some Versions of Pastoral.* 1935; rpt. New York: New Directions, 1950.

Ewing, Juliana Horatia. *A Great Emergency and a Very Well-Tempered Family.* New York: Schocken Books, 1969.

————. *The Story of a Short Life, Jackanapes, Daddy Darwin's Dovecot.* New York: A. L. Burt, n.d.

Fairchild, Hoxie Neale. *The Noble Savage: A Study in Romantic Naturalism.* Vol. 90 of Columbia University Studies in English and Comparative Literature. New York: Columbia University Press, 1928.

————. *Religious Trends in English Poetry.* Vol. 1: *1700–1740: Protestantism and the Cult of Sentiment;* Vol. 2: *1740–1780: Religious Sentimentalism in the Age of Johnson.* New York: Columbia University Press, 1939, 1942.

Ferguson, John. *Pelagius.* London: W. Heffer, 1956.

Fielding, Henry. *The Complete Works.* 18 vols. London: Frank Cass, 1967.

Fisher, Peter F. *The Valley of Vision: Blake as Prophet and Revolutionary.* Toronto: Toronto University Press, 1961.

Flugel, J. C., and West, Donald J. *A Hundred Years of Psychology, 1833–1933.* New York: Basic Books, 1964.

Forster, John. *The Life of Charles Dickens.* 2 vols. London: J. M. Dent, 1966.

Fotheringham, James. *Wordsworth's "Prelude" as a Study of Education.* 1899; rpt. Folcroft, Pennsylvania: Folcroft Press, 1969.

Fowler, W. Warde. *Social Life at Rome.* 1908; rpt. London: Macmillan, 1965.

Freud, Sigmund. *An Autobiographical Study.* Trans. James Strachey. 2nd ed.; Hogarth Press, 1946.

————. *The Ego and the Id.* Trans. Joan Riviere. 4th ed.; London: Hogarth Press, 1947.

————. *The Interpretation of Dreams.* Trans. James Strachey. New York: Basic Books, 1959.

Frye, Northrop. *Fearful Symmetry: A Study of William Blake.* Boston: Beacon Press, 1962.

Gardner, Emelyn E., and Ramsey, Eloise. *A Handbook of Children's Literature.* New York: Scott, Foresman, 1927.

George, M. Dorothy. *London Life in the Eighteenth Century.* New York: Capricorn Books, 1965.

Gignilliat, George Warren. *The Author of Sandford and Merton: A Life of Thomas Day.* Unnumbered volume in Columbia University Studies in English and Comparative Literature. New York: Columbia University Press, 1932.

Gilchrist, Alexander. *The Life of William Blake.* New York: Dodd, Mead, 1906.

Gillham, D. G. *Blake's Contrary States: The Songs of Innocence and Experience as Dramatic Poems.* Cambridge: Cambridge University Press, 1966.

Goldfarb, Russell M. "Charles Dickens: Orphans, Incest and Repression," in *Sexual Repression and Victorian Literature.* Lewisburg: Bucknell University Press, 1970, 111 38.

Gordon, E. V., ed. *Pearl.* Oxford: Clarendon Press, 1953.

Gordon, Jan B. "The *Alice* Books and the Metaphors of Victorian Childhood," in *Aspects of Alice: Lewis Carroll's Dreamchild as Seen Through the Critics' Looking-Glasses.* Robert Phillips ed. New York: Vanguard, 1971. 107–128.

Gosse, Edmund. *Father and Son: A Study of Two Temperaments.* London: William Heinemann, 1907.

—————. *The Life of Algernon Charles Swinburne.* Vol. 19 of *The Complete Works* (Bonchurch ed.). London: William Heinemann, 1927.

—————. *The Naturalist of the Sea-Shore: The Life of Philip Henry Gosse.* London: William Heinemann, 1896.

Grant, Philip. *The History of Factory Legislation.* Manchester: John Heywood, 1866.

Graves, Robert, and Hodge, Alan. *The Long Week-End: A Social History of Great Britain, 1918–1939.* 1940; rpt. New York: W. W. Norton, 1963.

Gray, Thomas. *The Complete Poems: English, Latin and Greek.* Eds. H. W. Starr and J. R. Hendrickson. Oxford: Clarendon Press, 1966.

Green, Roger Lancelyn. *Tellers of Tales.* 2nd ed.; Leicester: Edmund Ward, 1953.

Hamman, Andre. *Baptism.* New York: Alba House, 1967.

Hammond, J. L., and Hammond, Barbara. *Lord Shaftesbury.* London: Constable, 1923.

————. *The Town Labourer, 1760–1832: The New Civilization.* London: Longmans, Green, 1920.

Hanway, Jonas. *Letters to the Guardians of the Infant Poor.* London, 1767.

————. *A Sentimental History of Chimney-Sweepers in London and Westminster Shewing the Necessity of Putting Them Under Regulations to Prevent the Grossest Inhumanity to the Climbing Boys.* London, 1785.

Harnack, Adolf. *History of Dogma.* 7 vols. 3rd ed. Trans. Neil Buchanan. 1900; rpt. New York: Dover Books, 1961.

Harper, George C., Jr. "A Study of the Prose Works of Sir Edmund Gosse, 1872–1907." *Dissertation Abstracts,* 20 (1959), 2290–91.

Harper, George McLean. *William Wordsworth: His Life, Works and Influence.* 2 vols. 1929; rpt. New York: Russell and Russell, 1960.

Harper, George Mills. *The Neoplatonism of William Blake.* Chapel Hill: University of North Carolina Press, 1961.

Havelock, Eric A. *Preface to Plato.* Cambridge: Belknap Press, 1963.

Hearnshaw, L. S. *A Short History of British Psychology, 1840–1940.* New York: Barnes and Noble, 1964.

Hodder, Edwin. *The Life and Work of the Seventh Earl of Shaftesbury, K.G.* 3 vols. London: Cassell, 1888.

Holmes, Elizabeth. *Henry Vaughan and the Hermetic Philosophy.* New York: Russell and Russell, 1967.

Horace. *Odes and Epodes.* Ed. Paul Shorey. New York: Benj. H. Sanborn, 1919.

House, Humphrey. *The Dickens World.* Oxford: Oxford University Press, 1941.

Hürlimann, Bettina. *Three Centuries of Children's Books in Europe.* Trans. Brian W. Alderson. New York: World, 1968.

Huxley, Aldous. "Edward Lear," in *Essays Old and New.* London: Chatto and Windus, 1926, 140–146.

————. "Vulgarity in Literature" (1930), in *Collected Essays*. New York: Harper and Row, 1971, 103–115.

————. "A Wordsworth Anthology," in *On the Margin*. London: Chatto and Windus, 1923, 155–160.

Irenaeus. *Adversus Haereses*. Vol. 152 of *Sources Chrétiennes*. Ed. Adelin Rousseau. Paris: Editions du Cerf, 1969.

James, Henry. *Selected Literary Criticism*. Ed. Morris Shapira. New York: McGraw-Hill, 1965.

————. *The Turn of the Screw and The Aspern Papers*. New York: E. P. Dutton, 1960.

————. *What Maisie Knew*. New York: Oxford University Press, 1966.

Janeway, James. *A Token for Children: Being an exact account of the conversion, holy and exemplary lives and joyful deaths of several young children . . . To which is added A Token for the children of New England* [by Cotton Mather]. Boston, 1771.

Johnson, Edgar. *Charles Dickens: His Tragedy and Triumph*. 2 vols. Boston: Little, Brown, 1952.

Jones, Ernest. *The Life and Work of Sigmund Freud*. Ed. Stephen Marcus and Lionel Trilling. 1953–1955; abridged New York: Anchor Books, 1963.

Landa, Louis. "The Shandian Homunculus: The Background of Sterne's 'Little Gentleman,'" in *Restoration and Eighteenth-Century Literature*. Ed. Carroll Caruden. Chicago: University of Chicago Press, 1963. 49–68.

Lang, Andrew, ed. *The Nursery Rhyme Book*. 1897; rpt. New York: Dover Books, 1972.

Lear, Edward. *The Complete Nonsense of Edward Lear*. 1947; rpt. New York: Dover Books, 1951.

Leavis, F. R., and Leavis, Q. D. *Dickens the Novelist*. London: Chatto and Windus, 1970.

Leavis, F. R. *The Great Tradition: George Eliot, Henry James, Joseph Conrad*. London: Chatto and Windus, 1962.

————. "*What Maisie Knew:* A Disagreement." *Scrutiny*, 17 (Summer 1950), 115–127.

Legouis, Pierre. *Andrew Marvell: Poet, Puritan, Patriot*. 1928; trans. New York: Oxford University Press, 1965.

Leishman, J. B. *The Art of Marvell's Poetry.* New York: Funk and Wagnalls, 1966.

Leslie, Shane. "Lewis Carroll and the Oxford Movement." *London Mercury,* 28 (July 1933), 233–239.

Lewes, George Henry. "Consciousness and Unconsciousness." *Mind,* 2 (April 1877), 156–167.

Lindsay, Jack. *Charles Dickens.* London: Andrew Dakers, 1950.

Literary World. Unsigned review of *What Maisie Knew.* Vol. 28 (December 1897), 454–455.

Locke, John. *The Educational Writings of John Locke: A Critical Edition.* Ed. James L. Axtell. Cambridge: Cambridge University Press, 1968.

————. *An Essay Concerning Human Understanding.* 2 vols. Ed. Alexander Campbell Fraser. Oxford: Clarendon Press, 1894.

MacLean, Kenneth. *John Locke and English Literature of the Eighteenth Century.* New Haven: Yale University Press, 1936.

Mannheim, Leonard. "The Dickens Hero as Child." *Studies in the Novel,* 1 (Summer 1969), 189–195.

Marcus, Steven. *Dickens: From Pickwick to Dombey.* New York: Basic Books, 1965.

Marshall, Dorothy. *The English Poor in the Eighteenth Century.* London: George Routledge and Sons, 1926.

Marvell, Andrew. *The Poems and Letters of Andrew Marvell.* 2 vols. Ed. H. M. Margoliouth. Oxford: Clarendon Press, 1927.

Matheson, Annie. "George Eliot's Children." *Macmillan's Magazine,* 46 (October 1882), 488–497.

Mayhew, Henry. *London Labour and the London Poor.* 4 vols. Ed. John D. Rosenberg. New York: Dover Books, 1968.

Meigs, Cornelia, et al. *A Critical History of Children's Literature: A Survey of Children's Books in English from Earliest Times to the Present.* New York: Macmillan, 1953.

Mercator, Marius. *Monuments Ad Pelagianam Nestorianamque Haeresim Pertinentia.* Vol. 48 of *Patrologia Latinae.* Paris: J.-P. Migne, 1862.

Meredith, George. *Poetical Works.* Ed. G. M. Trevelyan. New York: Scribner, 1928.

Mill, John Stuart. *Autobiography*. New York: Columbia University Press, 1944.

———. "Nature," in *English Prose of the Victorian Era*. Eds. Charles F. Harrold and William D. Templeman. New York: Oxford University Press, 1938, 727–751.

———. *A System of Logic*. London: Longmans, 1961.

Miller, Robert P. "Chaucer's Pardoner, The Scriptural Eunuch, and the Pardoner's Tale." *Speculum,* 30 (1955); in *Chaucer Criticism*. Eds. Richard Schoeck and Jerome Taylor. Notre Dame: Notre Dame Books, 1960, 221–244.

Milton, John. *Complete Poems and Major Prose*. Ed. Merritt Y. Hughes. New York: Odyssey Press, 1957.

Misch, Georg. *A History of Autobiography in Antiquity*. 2 vols. Trans. E. W. Dickes. 1907; rpt. London: Routledge and Kegan Paul, 1950.

Monroe, Paul. *A Textbook in the History of Education*. 1905; rpt. New York: AMS Press, 1970.

Montgomery, James, ed. *The Chimney-Sweeper's Friend and Climbing-Boy's Album*. London: Longman, Hurst, Rees, Orme, Brown, and Green, 1824.

Moorman, Mary. "Wordsworth and His Children," in *Bicentenary Wordsworth Studies in Memory of John Alban Finch*. Ed. Jonathan Wordsworth. Ithaca: Cornell University Press, 1970, 111–141.

More, Thomas. *The History of King Richard III*. Vol. 2 of *The Complete Works*. Ed. Richard S. Sylvester. New Haven: Yale University Press, 1963.

Morris, John N. *Versions of the Self*. New York: Basic Books, 1966.

Moxon, Reginald Stewart. *The Doctrine of Sin*. London: Allen and Unwin, 1922.

Newman, John Henry. *An Essay on the Development of Christian Doctrine*. New York: Longman, Green, 1906.

Orwell, George. "Charles Dickens" (1939), *A Collection of Essays*. Garden City, N.Y.: Doubleday-Anchor, 1954, 55–111.

———. "Nonsense Poetry." *Shooting an Elephant and Other Essays*. New York: Harcourt, Brace, 1950, 114–120.

Packer, Lona M. *Christina Rossetti.* Berkeley: University of California Press, 1963.

Pater, Walter. *The Child in the House,* in *English Prose of the Victorian Era.* Eds. Charles F. Harrold and William D. Templeman. New York: Oxford University Press, 1938, 1469–1478.

Patrides, C. A. *Milton and the Christian Tradition.* Oxford: Clarendon Press, 1966.

*The Pearl: A Journal of Facetiae and Voluptuous Reading.* Nos. 1–18 (July 1879–December 1880). Rpt. New York: Grove Press, 1968.

Pfeiffer, John Richard. "The Child in Nineteenth Century British Fiction and Thought: A Typology." *Dissertation Abstracts,* 31 (1970), 1238-A (University of Kentucky).

Philips, Ambrose. *The Poems of Ambrose Philips.* Oxford: Basil Blackwell, 1937.

Pinney, Thomas. "George Eliot's Reading of Wordsworth: The Record." *Victorian Newsletter,* 24 (Fall 1963), 2–23.

Plato. *The Laws.* Vol. 2 of *The Dialogues of Plato.* Trans. Benjamin Jowett. 1871; rpt. Oxford: Oxford University Press, 1964.

———. *Plato's Cosmology: The Timaeus of Plato.* Trans. Francis M. Cornford. 1937; rpt. New York: Bobbs-Merrill, n.d.

Plutarch. *Moral Essays.* Trans. Rex Warner. Harmondsworth: Penguin Books, 1971.

Pohle, Joseph. *The Sacraments.* 2 vols. London: B. Herder, 1931.

Pope-Hennessy, Una. *Charles Dickens.* New York: Howell, Soskin, 1946.

Quintilian. *De Institutione Oratoria.* Vol. 1. Cambridge: Harvard University Press, 1953.

Rader, Melvin. *Wordsworth: A Philosophical Approach.* Oxford: Clarendon Press, 1967.

Rank, Otto. *The Myth of the Birth of the Hero and Other Writings,* Trans. F. Robbins and Smith Ely Jelliffe. New York: Vintage Books, 1964.

Roe, F. Gordon. *The Victorian Child*. London: Phoenix House, 1959.

Rossetti, Christina. *The Poetical Works of Christina Georgina Rossetti*. Ed. William Michael Rossetti. London: Macmillan, 1904.

Røstvig, Maren-Sofie. *The Happy Man: Studies in the Metamorphoses of a Classical Ideal; 1660–1700:* No. 2 in Oslo Studies in English. Oslo: Oslo University Press, 1954.

Rousseau, Jean Jacques. *Emile, Julie and Other Writings*. Trans. R. L. Archer. Woodbury, N.Y.: Barron's Educational Series, 1964.

———. *Emile*. Trans. William Boyd. New York: Teachers College Press, 1960.

———. *The Minor Educational Writings*. Trans. William Boyd. New York: Teachers College Press, 1962.

Sadler, Michael. *Thomas Day: An English Disciple of Rousseau*. Cambridge: Cambridge University Press, 1928.

Santayana, George. "Dickens," in *Soliloquies in England and Later Soliloquies*. New York: Constable, 1922, 58–72.

———. *Interpretations of Poetry and Religion*. 1900; rpt. New York: Harper and Brothers, 1957.

Sewell, Elizabeth. *The Field of Nonsense*. London: Chatto and Windus, 1952.

Shaftesbury, the Seventh Earl of. [Anthony Ashley]. "Infant Labour." *Quarterly Review*, 67 (December 1840), 171–181.

Sherwood, Mary Martha. *The History of the Fairchild Family*. London: James Nisbet, n.d.

Shumaker, Wayne. *English Autobiography*. No. 8 in University of California Publications: English Studies. Berkeley: University of California Press, 1954.

Simeral, Isabel. *Reform Movements in Behalf of Children in England of the Early Nineteenth Century, and the Agents of Those Reforms*. New York: privately printed, 1916.

Simon, Irène. "Innocence in the Novels of George Eliot." *English Studies Today*, 2nd series. Ed. G. A. Bonnard. Berne: Francke Verlag, 1961, 197–215.

Stephen, Leslie. *George Eliot*. New York: Macmillan, 1902.

Sterne, Laurence. *The Life and Opinions of Tristram Shandy, Gentleman.* Ed. James Aiken Work. New York: Odyssey Press, 1940.

———. *The Sermons of Mr. Yorick.* 2 vols. New York: Clonmel Society, 1904.

Stewart, Stanley. *The Expanded Voice: The Art of Thomas Traherne.* San Marino, California: Huntington Library, 1970.

Stokes, Ella Harrison. *The Conception of a Kingdom of Ends in Augustine, Aquinas, and Leibniz.* Chicago: University of Chicago Press, 1912.

Summers, Joseph H. "Marvell's 'Nature.'" *ELH,* 20 (1953), 121–135.

Tennant, F. R. *The Sources of the Doctrines of the Fall and Original Sin.* 1903; rpt. New York: Schocken Books, 1968.

Tertullian. *De Baptismo.* Vol. 35 of *Sources Chrétiennes.* Ed. R. F. Refoulé. Paris: Editions du Cerf, 1952.

Thomas, Katherine Elwes. *The Real Personages of Mother Goose.* Boston: Lothrop, Lee and Shepard, 1930.

Traherne, Thomas. *Centuries, Poems, and Thanksgivings.* 2 vols. Ed. H. M. Margoliouth. Oxford: Clarendon Press, 1958.

Trilling, Lionel. *The Liberal Imagination.* New York: Viking, 1951.

———. "Wordsworth and the Rabbis," in *The Opposing Self.* New York: Viking, 1955, 118–150.

Tuchman, Barbara W. *The Proud Tower: A Portrait of the World Before the War, 1890–1914,* New York: Macmillan, 1966.

Vaughan, Henry. *The Complete Poetry.* Ed. French Fogle. New York: W. W. Norton, 1964.

Vries, Leonard de. *Little Wide-Awake: An Anthology from Victorian Children's Books and Periodicals.* London: Arthur Barker, 1967.

Walsh, William. "Coleridge's Vision of Childhood." *The Listener,* 53 (February 1955), 336–340.

Watts, Isaac. *The Poems of Watts.* 2 vols. Chiswick: C. Whittingham, 1822.

Welsh, Alexander. "Satire and History: The City of Dickens." *Victorian Studies,* 11 (March 1968), 379–403.

Willen, Gerald, ed. *A Casebook on Henry James's The Turn of the Screw*. New York: Thomas Y. Crowell, 1960.

Willey, Basil. *More Nineteenth Century Studies: A Group of Honest Doubters*. New York: Columbia University Press, 1956.

————. "Wordsworth and the Locke Tradition," in *The Seventeenth Century Background*. London: Chatto and Windus, 1934, 226–277.

Williams, Norman Powell. *The Ideas of the Fall and of Original Sin*. London: Longmans, Green, 1927.

Wilson, Angus. "Dickens on Children and Childhood," in *Dickens 1970*. Ed. Michael Slater. New York: Stein and Day, 1970, 195–227.

————. *The World of Charles Dickens*. New York: Viking, 1970.

Wilson, Edmund. "The Two Scrooges," in *The Wound and the Bow*. Boston: Houghton Mifflin, 1941, 1–104.

Woolf, Virginia. "Edmund Gosse." *Fortnightly Review*, 135 (June 1, 1931), 766–773.

————. "'I Am Christina Rossetti,'" in *The Second Common Reader*. New York: Harcourt, Brace, 1932, 257–265.

————. "Lewis Carroll," in *The Moment and Other Essays*. New York: Harcourt, Brace, 1948.

Wordsworth, William. *Poetical Works*. Ed. Thomas Hutchinson. 2nd ed. London: Oxford University Press, 1936.

Young, George M., ed. *Early Victorian England: 1830–1865*. 2 vols. London: Oxford University Press, 1934.

# Index

Absurdism: and the child's perspective, 119–21, 147–51; in *David Copperfield*, 126; in Lewis Carroll, 157–59

Allegory, 85

Anglican Church. *See* Church of England

Apocalypse, the, 68, 99

Aquinas, Thomas, 19, 41, 159

Arian heresy, 11

Aristotle, 1–2, 8, 33

*Athenaeum*, 139

Augustine, Saint: and the doctrine of Original Sin, 11–20 passim, 52; *Confessions*, 17–18, 108–9, 110–11, 114; concept of childhood, 17–19, 118–19, 147; and English literature, 25, 26, 42, 64, 84, 86, 87, 99, 136; and Freud, 106, 111; mentioned, 21, 38–39, 45, 81, 93, 95, 100, 159. *See also* Original Sin

Austen, Jane, 94

Autobiography: and Original Sin, 18; as a genre, 108–10, 112; childhood in, 110–21 passim

Balfour, Arthur, 115

Baptism: replaces circumcision, 11; infant baptism and Original Sin, 15–17, 162n17; and the child figure, 21–22, 23, 41–42, 64, 91–92, 98–99; mentioned, 57, 125. *See also* Original Sin

Blake, William: and the language of childhood, 30; *Songs of Inno-cence and Experience*, 65–69; on nature and the Fall, 100–101, 165n18; mentioned, 79, 128

Browning, Robert, 113

Buckingham, George Villiers, second Duke of, 29

Bunyan, John, 78, 135

Byron, George Gordon, Lord, 113, 142

Caelestius the heretic, 11–12

Caesar, Julius, 109

Calvin, John, 42–44, 92

Calvinism, 97

Carlyle, Thomas, 76, 92, 115

Carroll, Lewis: *Alice in Wonderland*, 23, 120, 151–59; and the Church of England, 139; *Through the Looking-Glass*, 152, 153, 154; *Symbolic Logic*, 156–59; mentioned, 25

Carthage, Council of, 17, 18, 39, 46, 69

Cato the Elder, 2

Chaucer, Geoffrey, 21, 80–81, 97

Chear, Abraham, 137, 139

Child Figure: discussed generally, 44–46. *See also specific authors and subjects*

Child molestation, 126

Child welfare legislation, 70

Chimney-sweepers, 65–67, 73–74

Christianity: and the Fall, 4–5; concept of innocent childhood in, 7–11 passim, 118–19; and Original Sin, 11–20 passim; and the

185

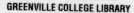